Millionaire Dropouts

Millionaire Dropouts Biography Edition

Biographies of the World's Most Successful Failures

Woody Woodward

www.MillionaireDropouts.com

D.U. Publishing
39252 Winchester Road #107-430
Murrieta CA 92563
admin@dupub.com
www.dupub.com

Millionaire Dropouts™ is trademark of Steven B. Woodward.

Warning—Disclaimer

ISBN-10: 0-9785802-4-9
ISBN-13: 978-0-9785802-4-7

PRINTED IN USA

Dedication

To the cynics who stopped believing in their dreams because someone once told them they couldn't do something and they believed that.

For those of us who are entrepreneurs, dreamers and builders who have always known we can. We didn't ask for permission. We made things happen by paying no attention to the critics.

Contents

Definition

$ $

dropout: 1. Anyone who gives up on an activity or goal.
2. Anyone who drops out of school or conventional society.

Millionaire Dropouts

Introduction

HAVE YOU EVER wondered how someone can drop out out of school and with very little money become successful? Many have overcome such odds. The first American millionaire and billionaire were dropouts. The first female African-American millionaire was a dropout.

Millionaire Dropouts started as a who's who of dropouts. Seven books later it has developed into an extensive list of great men and women who overcame obstacles and beat the odds to succeed. Founders of some of the greatest companies and people responsible for some of the most important inventions of modern times had little formal education. How can someone without a degree and starting with little money go on to build empires? It is the age-old question: What drives one person to success while another stops at failure? In this volume you will find the biographies of many people who have beaten the odds to become successful. You may recognize a few. You may work for one of them.

For a complete list of dropouts and for additional information, please visit www.MillionaireDropouts.com.

Biographical Sketches

O N THE FOLLOWING pages you will find brief biographical sketches of billionaire and millionaire dropouts who have gone before you. Some are historical figures and others are very much alive today. They all have lessons to teach by their examples.

Of the handful of billionaires in the world, a remarkable percentage are dropouts. That's why I've started with them, followed by a few people who were millionaires when millionaires were as rare as billionaires are today. The rest of the individuals are grouped roughly according to what they did to become millionaires.

I hope you enjoy reading about them.

Millionaire Dropouts Trivia

The richest man in the world thirteen years running, Bill Gates, with a net worth of $50 billion, is a dropout.

Billionaires

Billionaires

Billionaires

Billionaires

Billionaires

Billionaires

Billionaires

Billionaires

Billionaires

10

David Geffen

BIRTH NAME David Geffen

BORN February 21, 1943

DROPPED OUT University of Texas at Austin

A POWERFUL NEW Hollywood mogul, David Geffen has lived an extraordinary life, his fortunes rising and falling with his career. He has remained upbeat through it all and has come back better and stronger after each setback. Born in Brooklyn, New York, to Ukrainian immigrants Abraham and Batya Geffen, David learned basic business skills from his parents, who manufactured and sold bras. He was not interested in school from an early age but was fascinated by music and movies. David joined the University of Texas at Austin but dropped out to follow his dream to make a name in the entertainment industry.

Geffen's first job was as an usher at the CBS-TV studios, but he soon landed a job at the William Morris Agency, the largest and most prestigious talent agency of the time. Within a few years, he earned the reputation of being their hottest agent. He joined Ashley Famous Agency in 1968, when they offered him $1,000 per week. Geffen was responsible for bringing together Neil Young with Crosby, Stills and Nash for their Woodstock performance.

In Los Angeles, his mentor, Ahmet Ertugen from Atlantic Records suggested he start his own label. In 1971 Geffen formed Asylum Records. Some of the artists he signed became top-selling musicians of the 1970s, including newcomers like Jackson Browne and the Eagles and established musicians like Bob Dylan, Linda Ronstadt and Joni Mitchell.

In 1972, Geffen sold Asylum Records to Warner Bros. and for the next few years tried his hand at different ventures, eventually opening the nightclub Roxy. He became vice chairman of Warner Brothers Pictures. After clashing with the chairman, Ted Ashley, Geffen was sent to New York as an executive assistant to Steve Ross.

These years were a low point in his life as he was also misdiagnosed with bladder cancer.

The early 1980s were more rewarding. In 1980 Geffen formed Geffen Records and signed musicians like Donna Summer and John Lennon. Two days after the release of his album *Double Fantasy*, John Lennon was killed. The album sold millions and became a money-spinner for Geffen Records. Elton John was the third artist Geffen signed to the new label. In 1987 the company signed Guns N' Roses and later Nirvana, changing people's perception that the company only promoted "tired" artists. During the same decade, Geffen diversified, producing Broadway musicals like *Dreamgirls* and *Cats* and movies like *Personal Best*, *Risky Business* and *Little Shop of Horrors*. He sold Geffen Records to MCA in 1990, for an estimated $550 million, becoming the first self-made billionaire in Hollywood.

Geffen was now a bona fide Hollywood mogul and in 1994 founded DreamWorks SKG, with Steven Spielberg and Jeffery Katzenberg. The studio produced several successful and award-winning films, including *Saving Private Ryan*, *American Beauty* and *Shrek*.

Geffen has a magnetic personality that his former roommate Joni Mitchell immortalized in her song "Free Man in Paris." Over the years he has been linked to famous woman including Marlo Thomas and Cher. In 1992 he publicly acknowledged he was gay after being pressured by gay rights activists to come forward.

David Geffen is seen as a man who held nothing sacred in his quest to become rich. He has often forsaken relationships to reach his goals. After his incredible climb to wealth, he learned that money isn't everything, it can't buy happiness.

$ **Millionaire Dropouts Trivia** $

Titanic, the highest grossing movie of all time, was directed by a dropout (James Cameron); and the two lead actors were dropouts (Leonardo Di Caprio and Kate Winslet).

H. Wayne Huizenga

BIRTH NAME Harry Wayne Huizenga
BORN December 29, 1937
DROPPED OUT Calvin College

WAYNE HUIZENGA IS the cofounder of Waste Management, Inc., the largest waste management firm in the world. He is also the man who made Blockbuster Video a household name, opening a new store approximately every 17 hours in the early 1990s. Huizenga is known to some as a ruthless businessman and to others as an intuitive strategist, being able to combine practical business knowledge with diplomatic skill.

Huizenga was born in Chicago into a family of Dutch immigrants who had started the first garbage collecting company of the city. His father, Harry Huizenga, a carpenter by trade, moved the family to Florida to capitalize on the real estate boom there. Wayne learned to disregard the turmoil in his parents' relationship and performed well in school, taking part in sports and school politics. He entered Calvin College, in Michigan, in 1956, but dropped out less than two years later. He trained with the Army Reserves for six months, got married and moved back to Fort Lauderdale, joining Pompano Carting, a waste disposal company.

With real estate booming and new houses and suburbs being constructed, garbage collection was a lucrative business. Huizenga convinced Wilbur Porter, of Porter's Rubbish Service, to sell him a truck and a list of customers in 1962. Over the next seven years, he expanded his business to become one of the largest in the area.

In his drive to succeed, Huizenga developed obsessive work habits, which often led to him venting his anger and frustrations on others, allegedly including his wife, Joyce. After six years of marriage, she filed for divorce, citing extreme cruelty to her and her two sons. In 1971, Huizenga married Marti Goldsby, a secretary at his firm, Southern Sanitation Service.

Seeing the growth potential in the waste collection business, Huizenga and Dean Buntrock formed Waste Management Inc., (WMI) in 1971. They consolidated the fractured industry by buying out smaller firms. Within the next ten years WMI became the largest waste disposal company in the world. Huizenga had become a business magnate through ambition and hard work. He retired in 1983 and purchased several service companies dealing in laundry, lawn care and pest control in Florida.

Huizenga first visited a Blockbuster video store in 1987 and was so impressed he decided to buy the company. Applying his standard procedures of targeting small firms, buying them outright or driving them out of business and then increasing the fees, he hiked the fees drastically at Blockbuster. Although his aggressive tactics led to a phenomenal growth in the company, Blockbuster has faced several lawsuits regarding discrimination over the years.

Huizenga was named as one of the ten most powerful people in the entertainment industry by *Entertainment Weekly* in 1994. After merging Blockbuster with Viacom in 1994 Huizenga started AutoNation, a nationwide auto dealership that offered a fixed price, and then a hotel chain called Extended Stay America.

In an effort to improve his image, Huizenga decided to invest in sports. He started a baseball team, naming them the Florida Marlins. In the following years, he also brought the Florida Panthers to town and then purchased the Miami Dolphins, becoming a folk hero in the region.

Ambition, restlessness and driving passion have made Wayne Huizenga what he is today. He bought companies, made them profitable and sold them for millions, making success look easy.

Steve Jobs

BIRTH NAME Steven Paul Jobs

BORN February 24, 1955

DROPPED OUT Reed College

STEVE JOBS, THE genius responsible for popularizing the concept of personal computers, is the co-founder and CEO of Apple Computers. Widely known for his passion for innovative technology and design, Jobs also drove the development of the wildly popular iPod.

Born in Los Altos, California, to unmarried parents, he was adopted by Paul and Clara Jobs and grew up in Mountain View, California. Steve showed keen interest in building things, solving problems and attending engineering lectures at Hewlett-Packard after school, even working there in the summer. After graduation from Homestead High School in 1972, he moved to Portland, Oregon, to enroll in Reed College; but he dropped out after one semester.

Returning to California, Jobs took a position as a technician at video game manufacturer Atari. In 1976, he co-founded Apple Computer, Inc., with Steve Wozniak, famously starting the company in a garage. They manufactured their first personal computer, Apple I, and sold it for $666. They introduced the updated Apple II in 1977, and it was successful in the home segment. In 1983, they introduced a new prototype, Lisa, with the first commercial graphical user interface and mouse. Although its price tag of $10,000 doomed it to failure in the market, it did create a demand that made the launch of the Macintosh, the following year, a tremendous success. Apple's progress was held back, as the operating systems used by the company differed in each of its initial computers, and these operating systems were not compatible with IBM computers that were dominating the market.

In 1984, with the launch of the Macintosh, it became possible for workers who had no programming background to begin using personal computers at the office. The ability to point, click and drag instead of typing commands at an operating system prompt changed forever the way people perceived computers.

After a power struggle with CEO John Sculley in 1985, Jobs was stripped of his powers and he resigned from the company. He went on to found NeXT, Inc., which made some breakthroughs in advancing computer technology, but their products were too expensive to be commercially viable.

Apple Computers purchased NeXT in 1996 for $402 million, making Jobs CEO in 1997. He took the company forward by branching out into the field of personal electronics with the iPod portable music player and iTunes. Jobs also focused on the power of branding and offered innovative designs in his computers.

In 1986, Jobs purchased Pixar Animation Studios from George Lucas. Pixar hit the big time a decade later with Toy Story and after that produced several award winning films, including Finding Nemo and The Incredibles.

Jobs married Laurene Powell in 1991. They live with their three children in Silicon Valley, close to where he grew up among the apple and apricot orchards. These orchards are where he got the name of his first company, Apple. Jobs remains a true innovator and diehard perfectionist. He once said, "Innovation distinguishes between a leader and a follower." He is reputed to be a great motivator although not necessarily a team player. A visionary who followed his dreams even at the cost of losing his company, Steve Jobs revolutionized the world by making personal computers available to the common man.

$ **Millionaire Dropouts Trivia** $

Asia's richest resident, Li Ka-shing, worth $18.8 billion, is a high school dropout.

Ray Kroc

BIRTH NAME Ray Kroc

BORN October 5, 1902

DIED January 14, 1984

DROPPED OUT High School

FOUNDER OF THE McDonald's Corporation, Ray Kroc revolutionized the fast food industry. *Time* quotes a Harvard Business School professor who described him as "the service sector's equivalent of Henry Ford."

Kroc was born in Oak Park, Illinois, in 1902. Eager to serve in World War I, he dropped out of school in 1917, lying about his age to become a Red Cross ambulance driver; but the war ended before he could be sent to Europe. He then found a job playing the piano on the radio, as he was an accomplished player.

In 1922, Kroc started selling cups for the Tulip Cup Company. While traveling, he met Earl Prince, inventor of a new Multimixer milkshake machine. Kroc was able to judge its sales potential and got the exclusive rights to sell the Multimixer. He was soon traveling across the U.S. promoting and selling it. In San Bernardino, California, he met the McDonald brothers, who ran a restaurant and had ordered eight Multimixers from him. Kroc was impressed with the efficient way they operated and offered to set-up nationwide franchises for them.

In 1955, Kroc opened his first McDonald's, just outside Chicago, and following the Mcdonald brothers' original low cost and low service approach he offered fast food at the lowest possible prices. In 1961, Kroc bought out the McDonald brothers for $2.7 million. By 1963, McDonald's had sold three billion burgers and had opened its 500th restaurant. Kroc established his 1000th restaurant in 1968 and was soon exploring expansion in Europe, opening his first restaurant there in 1971.

Kroc's decision to target children could not have been better timed. The baby boom led to McDonald's becoming an accepted part of an American family's life, with its child-centered menu, play zones and the new icon of the company, Ronald McDonald. The clown was to become so popular that for most children he was more recognizable than the U.S. president.

Seeing trends and shifts in popular culture ahead of others, Kroc offered Americans a place "to eat, not dine," a casual and friendly restaurant, where there was no waiting and no reservations. Kroc was well known for his dedication to high standards, offering "quality, service, cleanliness and value" under efficient leadership. He created a chain of restaurants that were almost identical across the world, while still maintaining the core principles of the company. A consummate salesman, Kroc changed the way Americans eat and what they think of fast food.

Kroc was named American of the Year in 1973. After retirement, he focused on charity work and sports. He became the owner of the San Diego Padres in 1974. Kroc died of a heart attack in 1984.

Ray Kroc never stopped innovating. He tried to open an upscale version of McDonalds; he set up tavern-themed restaurants and pie shops; but these ventures were not successful. He had a strong sense of trends, strongly believed in his vision and had an indefatigable drive to succeed. Although he did not invent fast food, he presented it in a novel way, winning the hearts of an entire generation.

$ **Millionaire Dropouts Trivia** $

Argentina's sole billionaire, Gregorio Perez, worth $1.7 billion, is a high school dropout.

John D. Rockefeller Sr.

BIRTH NAME John Davison Rockefeller

BORN July 8, 1839

DIED May 23, 1937

DROPPED OUT High School

JOHN D. ROCKEFELLER, the capitalist and renowned philanthropist who created Standard Oil, was born in Richford, New York to William A. and Eliza Davison Rockefeller. As a child, John lived in Monrovia and Owego, New York, before moving to Cleveland, Ohio, in 1853. He was a good student, excelling in math and on the debating team, both skills that helped him later in life. John's father was a traveling salesman; the main influence in John's life was his mother, who taught him to work hard, save money and donate to charities.

Leaving high school in 1855, Rockefeller enrolled in Folsom Mercantile College for a six-month business course, completing it in three months and joining commission merchant firm Hewitt & Tuttle as a bookkeeper. By 1859, he started a commission business in partnership with Maurice B. Clark. The partners invested in an oil refinery, as Cleveland was gaining stature as an important refining center.

Rockefeller, along with his brother William, Henry M. Flagler and others, formed The Standard Oil Company in 1870, with $1 million in capital. In two years, the company had bought all the small refineries in Cleveland. In addition to his interests in the oil industry, Rockefeller invested in iron mines, timber plantations and factories. He also played an important part in the establishment of Chase Manhattan Bank.

The Standard Oil Company controlled approximately 90 percent of petroleum production in the U.S. by 1879 and had set up a distribution system covering nearly every town in America. Standard was aggressive. The company engaged in practices that led to its unpopularity with competitors, but customers liked their low prices. Rockefeller built a network of companies under the Standard Oil Trust, which the public eventually came to see as evil, leading to the antitrust movement. In a landmark judgment in 1911, the Supreme Court declared Standard Oil to be a monopoly and ordered it broken up into smaller companies. A total of 34 new companies were formed including those that became Chevron, Exxon, Mobil and Conoco.

In 1896, Rockefeller retired from active involvement in Standard Oil, although he remained president of the company until 1911. He then focused on philanthropy. As a boy, he gave most of his earnings to the church, and the tradition of charity and helping others was deeply ingrained in him. He contributed and ensured others' donations to found the University of Chicago. In 1901, he set up the Rockefeller Institute for Medical Research, later named The Rockefeller University, to discover causes of diseases and how to prevent them. In another effort to improve education, he formed the General Education Board (GEB) to promote education without "distinction of race, sex or creed". The Rockefeller Sanitary Commission worked between 1909 and 1915 to eradicate hookworm disease in the south. The Rockefeller Foundation was formed in 1913 to "promote the well-being of mankind throughout the world". Rockefeller also made personal donations to several universities, theological schools, Baptist missionary organizations and YMCAs and YWCAs.

Rockefeller married Laura Celestia Spelman in 1864; they had four daughters and one son, John D. Jr, who inherited most of the family fortune. John D. Rockefeller Sr. died at his home in Ormond Beach, Florida in 1937.

Rockefeller was not in the business of making money. He followed his passion for work and his instinct to stay ahead of the times; money was a byproduct. He once said, "I believe the power to make money is a gift from God. ... Having been endowed with the gift I possess, I believe it is my duty to make money and still more money, and to use the money I make for the good of my fellow man according to the dictates of my conscience."

J.R. Simplot

BIRTH NAME John Richard Simplot
BORN January 9, 1909
DROPPED OUT High School

J.R. SIMPLOT IS the founder of the J.R. Simplot Company, one of the largest privately owned companies in the world. His company is famous for inventing the procedure to produce high quality frozen french fries and is the largest supplier of french fries to McDonald's. J.R. Simplot was born in Dubuque, Iowa, in 1909 to Charles Richard and Dorothy Simplot. The family lived in the Snake River valley in Idaho and J.R. dropped out of school in the eighth grade when he left home after fighting with his father.

In 1923, Simplot decided to go into business for himself. He leased 120 acres near Declo, Idaho, to grow potatoes. Observing that the market for hogs was down, he set up a hog feeding operation with his father's help. He fed over three hundred hogs through the winter, on potatoes he grew and wild horses he caught, and sold them the following spring for a $7,000 profit. He used that money to buy horses and more land to start potato farming in earnest. In 1928, He bought a potato sorting machine and by the start of World War II had became the largest potato farmer in Idaho, shipping out 5,000 rail cars per season. Simplot noticed the shortage of fertilizers during the war and built a manufacturing plant in Pocatello, Idaho. It was this quick thinking and problem solving, combined with ambition and restless energy that led to his tremendous success.

By branching out into potato and vegetable processing, Simplot capitalized on the huge market of supplying dehydrated onions and potatoes to the military. The company also mined iron ore, had a fish farm and supplied hamburger patties. In 1946, company chemist Ray Dunlap invented a process to make frozen french fries that would not turn soggy. This innovation revolutionized the way fast food companies like McDonald's functioned. An estimated 40 percent of the company's profit comes from supplying McDonald's with frozen french fries.

As a high school dropout, Simplot relied on intuition and common sense. As the company grew, he stayed in touch with the workings of his company, making sure he knew how to do the job himself before delegating it to someone else. A strong believer in rejuvenating the American West, he also invested in several unrelated projects, making sudden decisions based more on gut feelings than business acumen.

Simplot transferred his voting stock to his children in the early 1960s and in 1973 retired as president. His eldest son, Richard, died in 1993. His second son, Donald, was not interested in education and had married five times. His daughter, Gay, was more interested in looking after the civic affairs of the company. Only his youngest son, Scott, is actively involved in the business.

By the 1980s the company had lost its innovative edge and its larger divisions were not growing, although they were profitable. J.R. decided to make another offbeat investment. in a start-up company called Micron Technology Inc., which made memory chips. Surprising everyone, the company was successful and its stock became highly sought after. Simplot earned millions from that investment. He retired from the board of J.R. Simplot Company in 1994, making way for the new generation of Simplots.

J.R.'s contributions to the potato industry have been honored in the World Potato Congress and the Idaho Potato Hall of Fame. Currently, he lives in downtown Boise with his wife, Esther.

Not only was J.R. Simplot a leader himself but he also inspired others to lead with him rather than just follow. The continuing success of his company is a testament to the fighting spirit that he instilled in his employees. His is one of the great success stories of twentieth-century America.

Steven Spielberg

BIRTH NAME   Steven Allan Spielberg

BORN   December 18, 1946

DROPPED OUT   California State University, Long Beach

STEVEN SPIELBERG WAS born in Cincinnati, Ohio, and grew up in Haddonfield, New Jersey, and later Scottsdale, Arizona. Encouraged by his mother, Leah, Steven made his first film when he was 12; an eight-minute western titled *The Last Gun*. He was soon making longer and technically superior films, mostly based on World War II.

Spielberg enrolled in California State University at Long Beach to study English, after he was turned down twice for a film course at the University of Southern California. He got a job with Universal Studios, where he made a short film called *Amblin*; this won an award at the Atlanta Film Festival and got him a seven-year contract with the studio. During this time, Spielberg directed episodes of several TV shows, including *Marcus Welby MD, The Name of the Game* and *Colombo*. His first TV movie, *Duel,* got him noticed and led to more movies, such as *Something Evil* and *Sugarland Express,* which was his own project and won him an award for best screenplay at the Cannes Film Festival.

The movie *Jaws,* an adaptation of Peter Benchley's book, took Spielberg to the big leagues. It was an astounding success and Spielberg became Hollywood's golden boy. *Close Encounters of the Third Kind,* a sci-fi thriller, was his next film. His one and only failure was *1941,* a comedy set in wartime Pearl Harbor. From then on, Spielberg made one blockbuster after another, always experimenting and pushing audiences a little bit further each time. Some of his most successful movies include *Raiders of the Lost Ark, ET: The Extra Terrestrial, The Twilight Zone, Indiana Jones and the Temple of Doom, Poltergeist,* and *Gremlins*. Other well-received movies include *Empire of the Sun, Always, Hook* and *The Color Purple. Jurassic Park* featured awe-inspiring special effects and became, with its sequel, *The Lost World,* among the highest-grossing movies of all time.

The starkly portrayed emotional drama, *Schindler's List,* a story of a Nazi who risked his life to save Jews from extermination camps, was Spielberg's ten-year-long dream and one of his finest movies. He won Oscars for best picture and best director for it. In 1994, Spielberg set up Dreamworks, a multimedia production company, with fellow dropout David Geffen and Jeffrey Katzenberg.

Saving Private Ryan, a superbly crafted, large-scale World War II movie, showed the Normandy landing in great detail. Spielberg took over *AI: Artificial Intelligence* after the death of Stanley Kubrick and created the movie through a child's eyes. In the detective genre, Spielberg made *Minority Report* and *Catch Me If You Can.*

In 2002, Spielberg finally received a degree from California State University Long Beach, the same school he had dropped out of in 1969.

The aloofness of Spielberg's father had a major impact on his life and his movies; he often depicts characters with reluctant or absent fathers. Although Spielberg has been the favorite of audiences, critics have often remarked on the lack of emotional depth in his films and on their focus on action.

Steven Spielberg has become like the legendary King Midas, turning everything he touches to gold. He has been successful in a wide range of genres, reaching out to the hearts of millions with his breathtaking special effects. Spielberg is one of the most powerful men in the history of film and Hollywood's most successful director. He blends a childlike sense of wonder with expertly crafted techniques and special effects to awe, entertain and frighten audiences.

$ **Millionaire Dropouts Trivia** $

**There are 67 billionaires who are dropouts
and numerous millionaires.**

Millionaires

Millionaires

Millionaires

Millionaires

Millionaires

Millionaires

Millionaires

Millionaires

Millionaires

John Jacob Astor

BIRTH NAME Johann Jakob Astor
BORN July 17, 1763
DIED March 29, 1848
DROPPED OUT High School

JOHN JACOB ASTOR became one of America's wealthiest men in
the nineteenth century. He made a fortune in fur trading and real
estate, and his name is synonymous with financial success.

Astor was born in Walldorf, Germany. At 16 he left home and
his father's butcher shop to go to London, where his brother George
manufactured musical instruments. In London, John helped his
brother with sales as he learned English. He traveled to New York
in 1784, at the end of the Revolutionary War, to explore new markets
for musical instruments. There he worked in a butcher's shop and
also as a baker for a while, before he was introduced to the fur trade,
starting his own shop later in the decade.

Astor started exploring New York for fur and for business connections and also met fur traders from Montreal, Canada. In the
late 1780s, he set up a fur goods shop in New York and became a
leading businessman in the trade. He soon started shipping fur to
London and importing musical instruments on the returning ships.
He also greatly benefited by the Jay Treaty between Great Britain
and the new United States, which opened markets in Canada and
the Great Lakes region.

When he married Sarah Todd, who was more than willing to
help him, his business grew even larger. He started shipping fur, tea
and sandalwood to China, as American traders did not need permission to trade in ports monopolized by the East India Company.

In 1808, Astor established the American Fur Company and
its subsidiaries, the Pacific Fur Company and the Southwest Fur
Company.

Astor's trade suffered when, during the War of 1812, the British captured his trading posts. But five years later the U.S. Congress barred foreign traders from U.S. territories, and his business bounced back. It once again thrived in the area around the Great Lakes. The Astor House on Mackinac Island became the headquarters for the American Fur Company. When the demand for fur declined because of changing fashions, Astor, being a shrewd investor, turned to real estate and made a fortune in that business, too.

Astor retired from business in 1834 to devote his time to philanthropy. He founded the Astor Library in New York and built a poorhouse in Walldorf, where he was born. He also set up the first hotel that belonged to the Astor family. He took active part in the presidential campaign of Henry Clay and became close friends with well-known ornithologist John James Audubon and the writer Edgar Allan Poe.

At the time of his death in 1848, he left an estate estimated to be worth $20 million. John Jacob Astor's driving ambition and shrewd business acumen made him America's first multimillionaire.

Millionaire Dropouts Trivia

Spain's richest resident, Amancio Ortega, worth $14.8 billion, is a high school dropout.

Andrew Carnegie

BIRTH NAME Andrew Carnegie

BORN November 25, 1835

DIED August 11, 1919

DROPPED OUT Elementary School

BORN IN DUNFERMLINE, Scotland, into a weaver's family, Andrew Carnegie had a difficult childhood. The industrial revolution saw steam-powered looms force hand weavers out of jobs. Andrew's mother had to work to support the family; she opened a grocery shop and earned some extra money mending shoes. Andrew experienced what it meant to be poor. Watching his father beg for work, he decided early in life that making money would be his goal. His mother persuaded her husband that it would be better for the family to move to America to join other relatives already there. Borrowing £20, the family left for Pittsburgh in 1848.

William, Andrew's father, got a job in a cotton factory and Andrew himself started working as a bobbin boy in the same building. He was 13 and he earned $1.20 per week.

The Carnegie family valued education. Andrew took advantage of the offer of a local gentleman who invited working boys to borrow from his personal library. Carnegie took a new job, at $2.50 a week, as a messenger in a telegraph office, where he applied his ingenuity to further his education, by arranging to deliver messages to theatres and then staying to watch Shakespearean plays. He also attended to his job, becoming one of the few people who could accurately and quickly transcribe incoming telegraphy by ear. Thomas A. Scott, a superintendent at the Pennsylvania Railroad, noticed him and made Carnegie his private secretary and personal telegrapher, paying him $4 a week. Carnegie partnered with the inventor of the sleeping car, reaping huge profits from the sale of the cars to the railroad at the same time he rose in the railroad for speeding up rail service by introducing the sleeping cars. By the time the Civil War ended in 1865, Carnegie was superintendent of the western division of the railroad.

During the Civil War, Carnegie's old mentor, Scott, was the Assistant Secretary of War and brought Carnegie with him for a stint in Washington. Carnegie, a shrewd investor, put $40,000 into a Pennsylvania farm in 1864 and made over $1 million in dividends the following year, on the oil shipped from the farm.

With the end of the Civil War, the iron industry opened up and, sensing that it had great potential, Carnegie resigned from Pennsylvania Railroad. He set up a steel plant in Pittsburgh and put all his money into the business, starting mass production of steel rails for railroad lines. Carnegie Steel became the largest manufacturer of pig iron and steel-rails. When he purchased Homestead Steel Works in 1892, the Carnegie Steel Company was formed. The company grew. In 1901, Carnegie sold his holdings to J.P. Morgan for $480 million.

Carnegie firmly believed that the rich have a moral obligation to give away their fortunes. He wrote a book called *The Gospel of Wealth*, in which he said that all personal wealth beyond that required to fulfill the needs of one's family should be regarded as a trust fund to be used for the benefit of the community.

Having educated himself by reading books in libraries, Carnegie established over 1,600 libraries in the U.S. alone and many in other countries from Scotland to Fiji. In 1901, he donated $2 million to start the Carnegie Institute of Technology (now Carnegie Mellon University) in Pittsburgh. In 1902, he gave another $2 million to fund the Carnegie Institution in Washington. DC, and the same amount in 1901 to assist Scottish universities.

When he died in 1919, Carnegie had given away $350 million in his lifetime. In his will he left another $30 million to foundations, trusts and charities.

Charles Emory Culpeper

BIRTH NAME Charles Emory Culpepper

BORN May 11, 1874

DIED February 2, 1940

DROPPED OUT High School

CHARLES CULPEPER (he dropped the extra *p* from his name) was a man of extraordinary vision. He pioneered the bottling and marketing of Coca-Cola. He has left behind a legacy that supports charitable causes in education and medical research.

Charles Emory Culpepper was born in Rome, Georgia. He was one of nine children and grew up on a family farm near Rome. Charles dropped out of high school, but he was always resourceful and hard working. He worked as a clerk in a store and later became a salesman. He did various odd jobs and in 1899, he started selling Coca-Cola syrup to soda fountains in Philadelphia. In 1904, he started working full time as a salesman for the Coca-Cola Bottling Works of Newark and New York.

Thirteen years later, in 1917, Charles Culpeper bought the Newark and New York bottlers for $160,000, using borrowed funds. The two companies were later combined to form the Coca-Cola Bottling Company of New York. He took the company to new heights and, when he died in 1940, his stock in the company amounted to a major fortune.

Although he lived in Norwalk, Connecticut, from 1913 on, he always wanted to give back something to his home state of Georgia. He was a humanitarian and wanted to work for the betterment of mankind. He died February 2, 1940 and was buried at the West Union Baptist Church Cemetery, Curryville, Georgia. He had no children and left a will that said the fortune he left behind should be used to form a charitable foundation.

The Charles E. Culpeper Foundation was formed in 1940 with his personal fortune and it has contributed to various charitable causes.

At the end of 1998, the foundation had assets worth over $207 million. The same year, the foundation also granted aid close to $8.7 million for health, education, art and cultural development.

The Charles E. Culpeper Foundation of Connecticut and the Rockefeller Brothers Fund of New York merged 1 July 1999 to form the Rockefeller Brothers Fund Inc., with its investment assets at that time valued at $650 million. The Charles E. Culpeper Scholarships in Medical Science and the Charles E. Culpeper Biomedical Pilot Initiative, the two programs established under the Culpeper name, continue under the new name. Programs in health, education, arts and culture that formed a part of Culpeper's vision for the wellbeing of mankind are also being carried out under the new name.

Culpeper's life was an extraordinary one. One man's vision and exemplary zeal led to the formation of a foundation that has helped in funding research and aid in the field of medicine and education, leading to major breakthroughs in medical research. Although Culpeper did not finish his schooling, he valued education and research and contributed immensely to both fields, making the world a better place to live.

$ **Millionaire Dropouts Trivia** $

Three of the ten richest people in the world are dropouts:
number 1, Bill Gates, worth $50 billion;
number 6, Paul Allen, worth $22 billion;
number 10, Li Ka-shing, worth $18.8 billion.

Del Webb

BIRTH NAME Delbert Eugene Webb
BORN May 17, 1899
DIED July 4, 1974
DROPPED OUT High School

D EL WEBB WAS born in Fresno, California, to wealthy pioneers Ernest and Henrietta Webb. When his father went bankrupt in 1914, Del left high school after his freshman year to help support his family, working as a carpenter's apprentice. He was interested in baseball, an interest he picked up from his father, and played semi-pro ball while working as a carpenter through the 1920s.

Webb got typhoid fever in 1927 and moved to Phoenix to recuperate. He decided to focus all his energies on construction and set up a small firm in 1928. He built a solid and reliable business using tactics that had helped him in baseball—making bold decisions, relying on teamwork and producing a steady performance even under pressure. Soon, his company became known for its ability to develop large-scale, high-quality projects, winning contracts for Madison Square Garden and the Los Angeles County Museum of Art.

During World War II, the company demonstrated to the military its ability to construct entire communities on barren land. This experience helped the company take part in the postwar boom in construction.

Webb's innovative approach to problem solving during the war led him to meet a number of influential people like Howard Hughes, with whom he shared common interests in golf and flying, and for whom he did over $1 billion worth of business. Webb returned to his first love, baseball, to buy the New York Yankees with Al Tipping in 1945. In the twenty years they owned the team, the Yankees won the World Series ten times.

Webb's company built Bugsy Siegel's Flamingo Hotel in Las Vegas in 1946, starting the gambling boom there. Webb capitalized on the rush and soon became the largest gaming operator and private employer in Nevada. The Sahara was Webb's first hotel in Las Vegas. Soon his friend Howard Hughes purchased property, improving the image of the city as a reputable place. Webb was a skilled observer of social psychology and understood and targeted the elite subculture.

In 1960, the Del Webb Corporation opened Sun City in Phoenix; the retirement community became a phenomenal success. The company decided to focus on developing active adult communities and divest from the gaming and commercial interests in 1987. Webb concentrated on building larger homes, offering more recreational and club facilities, leading the way for providing a luxurious environment. The company built thirteen Sun Cities with over 80,000 homes, and its annual revenues grew to $2 billion when it merged with Pulte Homes in 2001, becoming the largest home construction company in the country.

Webb married his childhood sweetheart Hazel. They were divorced in 1952, and in 1961 he married Toni Ince. Webb died of lung cancer in 1974. As neither marriage produced any children, most of Webb's fortune went to the Del E. Webb Foundation, funding medical projects in Arizona, California and Nevada.

Del Webb, real estate developer and former owner of the New York Yankees was a self-made man. Following his twin passions of baseball and carpentry, he forged a company from nothing just as he built communities in the Arizona desert. He relied on his creative working style, attention to detail and positive attitude to create the largest construction company in the U.S. He was a man known for his integrity, values and a strong dedication to his commitments. He was always ahead of the curve, recognizing and paving the way for independent homes for adults, capitalizing on the postwar construction boom and using innovative marketing and problem solving techniques.

Founders

Founders

Founders

Founders

Founders

Founders

Founders

Founders

Founders

Wally Amos

BIRTH NAME Wallace Amos Jr.

BORN July 1, 1936

DROPPED OUT Food Trade Vocational
High School

WALLY AMOS IS the inventor of Famous Amos chocolate chip cookies and founder of the company that bears the same name. He is credited with being the father of the gourmet chocolate chip cookie industry. Known as an entrepreneur, orator, philosopher and author, Amos has used his success and fame to support literacy programs and other causes.

Wally Amos was born in 1936 in Tallahassee, Florida, and lived there with his parents till the age of 12. He then moved to New York City to live with his Aunt Della. With his interest in cooking, Amos decided to enter the Food Trades Vocational High School. When he was a senior, he dropped out to join the U.S. Air Force, where he completed his GED. This changed his life and made it possible for him to train at a secretarial school in New York after he was honorably discharged from the service.

On completion of his secretarial training, he started working in a clerical position at the William Morris Agency and became the agency's first African-American talent agent, representing musical acts like Simon and Garfunkel, Diana Ross and the Supremes.

Amos was innovative in his approach. He brought clients to the Agency by sending them chocolate chip cookies with invitations to visit him. After a few years, he decided to focus on what had till then been a weekend hobby, chocolate chip cookies. He began to sell cookies based on his Aunt Della's recipe. The first Famous Amos store opened in 1975 in Los Angeles.

Amos hosted a series of programs on PBS for adult basic learners. In 1977, he became an ardent advocate for literacy in America, and in 1979, he became the national spokesman for Literacy Volunteers of America. He also became a board member of the National Center for Family Literacy and Communities in schools.

After being hired by an influential firm as a professional speaker, Amos became known for his dynamic style and an inspiring and positive attitude. He extolled the principles that made him successful. By being humble and sharing his setbacks and unfulfilled dreams, he enabled his audiences to identify with him.

Amos has received several honors and awards. He gave the shirt off his back and his trademark battered Panama hat to be displayed at the Smithsonian Institution's Business Americana Collection. Johnson & Wales University awarded him an honorary doctorate in education. He was also inducted into the Babson College Academy of Distinguished Entrepreneurs. Other awards he has received are the Horatio Alger Award; The President's Award for Entrepreneurial Excellence and The National Literacy Honors Award.

In 1983, he wrote his autobiography, *The Famous Amos Story: The Face that Launched a Thousand Chips*. He also wrote *The Power in You: Ten Secret Ingredients to Inner Strength*; and *Man with No Name: Turn Lemons into Lemonade*, where he shares his experiences of losing everything he had, including his name, and overcoming adversities by turning them into opportunities. His last book, published in 1996, was *Watermelon Magic: Seeds of Wisdom, Slices of Life*, in which he uses a watermelon as a metaphor for life and shared his philosophy and insights.

Wally Amos lives in Maui, Hawaii, and is actively involved in public speaking, sharing his dreams and philosophy of life. He focused on his drive to succeed by trusting in his invincible spirit and positive approach to life. He is a firm believer in practicing what he preaches and knew all aspects of his business closely. Even though his is a household name, he remains grounded in reality and still maintains his trademark positive spirit.

William E. Boeing

BIRTH NAME William Edward Boeing
BORN October 1, 1881
DIED September 28, 1956
DROPPED OUT Yale University

WILLIAM BOEING, THE founder of the Boeing Airplane Co., was a pioneer in the American aviation industry. His passion for flying took the aviation industry in America to new heights.

Boeing was born in Detroit. He entered the Sheffield Scientific School at Yale University but dropped out two years later, in 1903, the year the Wright brothers flew at Kitty Hawk. Boeing moved to Washington, where he built a fortune trading timber lands, settling in Seattle in 1908. He attended a public air show in California, where he became fascinated with flying and the field of aviation. In 1914, he flew for the first time, but by then he knew he wanted to build his own plane. He was confident that he could come out with a better plane than the ones that were being used at the time.

Boeing worked with his friend George Conrad Westervelt, an engineer, to design the B&W, a twin-float seaplane. He started his own company, Pacific Aero Products Co., in 1916, changing the name to the Boeing Airplane Co. a year later. The company started manufacturing airplanes in a seaplane hanger in Seattle.

In 1917, Boeing had parts of a plane shipped off to Florida to be reassembled and displayed for Navy officials to test. Boeing anticipated that the U.S. Navy would need such planes for use in World War I. His hunch proved to be right and the Navy ordered 50 planes. After the war, however, the demand for planes declined and Boeing managed to keep his company going by diversifying into building furniture and boats.

The company came out with the B-1, a biplane that created history on March 3, 1919, when Boeing and pilot Eddie Hubbard flew the plane from Seattle to Vancouver. It was the first international airmail route. This service continued till the mid 1920s. Later, the company began building fighters. It started manufacturing engines and propellers as well. In 1934, Boeing received the Daniel Guggenheim Medal for successful pioneering and achievement in aircraft design and manufacturing.

In 1934, the U.S. government passed new federal laws that did not allow airmail carriers and aircraft manufacturers to be part of the same company. As orders were cancelled, William Boeing was forced to split his company into different companies. He later sold his stock in the company.

Boeing's interest in the aviation industry continued and he offered his services as a consultant to his former company during World War II. During the war the company produced the B-17, the B-29 and the Kaydet trainer. The B-17 Flying Fortress and the B-29 Super Fortress became the symbols of America's military pride. It was a Boeing B-29 Super Fortress that carried the first atomic bomb that was dropped on Japan. By the 1950s, with his health failing, William Boeing dissociated himself from the company's activities. By the time he died in 1956, the company he had founded had entered the jet age.

William Boeing set his dreams up in the sky. With his great vision, hard work and innovative ideas, his legacy in the American aviation industry is assured.

$ **Millionaire Dropouts Trivia** $

**Some of history's greatest companies
were founded by dropouts,
including Kodak, Polaroid, Famous Amos, Disney,
Ford, Learjet, Bank of America, Motown Records,
Whole Foods, Domino's, Apple Computer, Netscape,
Microsoft, Polo, Jet Blue, Dunkin' Donuts, NBC, KFC,
Wendy's, McDonald's, Holiday Inn
and Rolling Stone Magazine.**

Walt Disney

BIRTH NAME Walter Elias Disney

BORN December 5, 1901

DIED December 15, 1966

DROPPED OUT High School

WALT DISNEY, THE creator of Mickey Mouse, was a pioneer, an innovator and an artist whose Hollywood career lasted 43 years. David Low, the late British political cartoonist once called him "the most significant figure in graphic arts since Leonardo DaVinci."

Walt Disney was born in Chicago, Illinois. His family moved to Marceline, Missouri, soon after Walt's birth and that was where he grew up. Interested in drawing from an early age, he drew small sketches to sell to his neighbors. His father, Elias Disney, was a strict disciplinarian. His mother, Flora Call Disney, and his brother Roy, however, encouraged him in his early years; and Walt grew up appreciating nature and wildlife. He went to McKinley High School in Chicago, where he studied both photography and drawing. He also attended the Academy of Fine Arts at night. The family later moved to Kansas City.

In 1918, Disney tried to enlist for military service but was rejected because he was only 16. So he joined the Red Cross and served in France, driving an ambulance and chauffeuring Red Cross officials. After his return from France, he started making short animated films. He ran out of money at around this time and, armed with a few drawing materials, $40 in his pocket and a copy of his film *Alice Comedies*, he left Kansas City for Hollywood. His brother Roy was already in California. Together they pooled their resources, borrowed $500 and started their production operations. After introducing Mickey Mouse in a couple of silent cartoons, Disney showed a synchronized sound version of *Steamboat Willie* at the Colony Theatre in New York on November 18, 1928, to great acclaim.

In 1932, *Flowers and Trees* won him his first Academy Award. In 1937, he made *The Old Mill*, using the multiplane camera technique for the first time. His first full-length animated musical feature *Snow White and the Seven Dwarfs* premiered at the Carthay Circle Theatre in Los Angeles. Produced at a cost of $1.5 million at the time of the Great Depression, it is considered a remarkable feat in the motion picture industry. Tragedy struck when, after the film's success, Walt moved his parents to a home close to his studio and his mother died of asphyxiation caused by a faulty furnace.

Disney went on to create animated classics such as *Pinocchio, Fantasia, Dumbo* and *Bambi*. His Burbank studio, built in 1940, had more than 1,000 artists, animators and technicians. Disney retained his interest in wildlife footage, too. Through his award winning series *True-Life Adventures*, he highlighted the importance of conserving nature.

Disneyland, opened in 1955, and was the original giant theme park. It borrowed ideas from some older-style amusement parks and smaller theme parks, but the size and originality made it a new phenomenon in the world. Disney's fanatical attention to production values and to cleanliness made the park a wholesome place for family vacations.

In thinking about the world, Disney found that the greatest challenge was to find solutions to problems faced by urban dwellers. With the idea of building a community that would become a prototype for the future, he built EPCOT Center (Experimental Prototype Community of Tomorrow), which opened on October 1, 1982, in Orlando, Florida. It is the heart of Walt Disney World Resort. The Disney-MGM Studios Theme Park opened on May 1, 1989. Walt Disney also established the California Institute of the Arts.

Winner of 48 Academy Awards, 7 Emmys and over 950 honors and citations, Walt Disney was a man whose contribution to the motion picture industry and the art of animation remains unsurpassed.

Amadeo Giannini

BIRTH NAME Amadeo Peter Giannini
BORN May 6, 1870
DIED June 3, 1949
DROPPED OUT High School

AMADEO GIANNINI FOUNDED Bank of America and is a pioneer of modern banking practices. He was the first man to come up with the unique concept of offering bank loans to poor immigrants. His sound business skills, liberal policies and innovative approach helped Bank of America become the largest banking network in America.

Amadeo Peter Giannini was born in San Jose, California, to Italian immigrant parents. When he was a small boy he saw his father killed by a man over a dollar. His widowed mother married Lorenzo Scatena, who was in the produce business. Amadeo dropped out of school to help his stepfather in his business. He worked hard and his stepfather was so impressed with him that he made Giannini a partner in the business when he was only 19 years old. In 1904, at the age of 31, he retired from the business. Being a fair-minded and honest man, Amadeo sold half the business to his employees. He had enough money and could have retired, but Giannini was a man of great vision.

He approached a few investors and, combining their money with his own, he started the Bank of Italy in 1904. In those days, loans were reserved for the rich and the creditworthy. Giannini came up with the revolutionary idea of offering loans to hardworking immigrants who were in need of money. Although home mortgages and auto loans are a common feature in any bank today, Giannini was the first person to offer such services in those days. He explained his ideas and convinced the immigrants to take loans, as they did not know much about banking. He built his business from scratch.

The Bank of Italy opened its doors October 17, 1904, with deposits of $8,780 on the first day.

After the 1906 San Francisco earthquake, most other banks closed; but Giannini rushed to his bank, gathered all the money, securities and gold and rushed out. He managed bank transactions on the street by placing a plank across two barrels and using it as a counter. He granted loans to people to rebuild their lives and helped reconstruct the city after the earthquake.

As his customers had to travel long distances to reach the bank, he started a branch in San Jose in 1909. He later opened several branches across the state and a few branches in other major cities across America. Thus began the first statewide banking system in the U.S. He started a holding company called Transamerica Corp. in 1928 and bought banks throughout New York, Washington, Arizona, Oregon and Nevada. He consolidated all the banks under one name—Bank of America. By 1945, despite the Great Depression, the Bank of America had grown to be the largest bank in the U.S. and the largest privately owned bank in the world.

Giannini's liberal lending policy also encouraged the agriculture sector and the motion picture industry to borrow. A generous man, he started the Bank of America–Giannini Foundation for Medical Research and Educational Scholarships. He also started the Giannini Foundation of Agricultural Economics at the University of California.

Giannini died in 1949, at the age of 79. He could have retired at 31, but his innovative ideas and great vision gave the world its largest banking network, helping ordinary, middle class and working class people build their lives and their dreams, too.

Soichiro Honda

BIRTH NAME Soichiro Honda

BORN November 17, 1906

DIED August 5, 1991

DROPPED OUT High School

SOICHIRO HONDA IS the man behind the success of the Honda Motor Company. Passionate about bikes and racing from a young age, he was instrumental in building a company that today produces the largest number of motorcycles.

Honda was born in the town of Komyo (now Tenryu) in Japan. His father was a blacksmith who also repaired bicycles. When he was young, Soichiro used to help his father in the garage.

Honda went to Tokyo in search of a job when he was 15 years old. He worked in a garage as an apprentice and later as a mechanic in an auto repair company for a few years before returning to his hometown to start his own mechanic business in 1928, at the age of 22.

Honda loved racing and took part in many racing competitions. He built his own race car using an old aircraft engine and assorted parts. In 1936, he broke several bones in a crash and stopped racing at his wife's urging.

In 1937, Honda started his own company, the Tokai Seiki Heavy Industry, to manufacture piston rings. Feeling that he had to learn a lot about casting, he went to a technical high school and applied the theories he learned there to his own factory. He did not take the exams at the end of the year though, for he did not believe in exams and certificates. Aircraft propellers mass-produced at the factory were of great help to Japanese troops during World War II. In 1948, he sold the company to Toyota for ¥450,000.

Honda started the Honda Technical Laboratory in Hamamatsu after the war. The company became known for its auxiliary bicycle engines. On September 24, 1948, the Honda Motor Company was formally established with an investment of ¥1 million. It started manufacturing engines and soon came out with the powerful Type E motorcycles, with an innovative valve design. The company expanded its operations and, in 1958, came out with the C 100 Super Cub, which became a bestseller worldwide. With the slogan "You meet the nicest people on a Honda," Honda motorcycles entered the American market in 1959.

Honda was still enthusiastic about motor racing and, in 1959, the company took part in the Isle of Man Tourist Trophy, winning the manufacturer's prize. Two years later, at the same motorcycle racing competition, Honda rode away with prizes in both the 125 cc and 250 cc categories. Honda became a household name and its exports skyrocketed. In 1965, the company entered the Formula 1 racing series. It won the Mexican Grand Prix and, a year later, won several races in the Formula 2 series.

Honda was the President of the Honda Motor Company till he retired in 1973, at the age of 67. He stayed on as its director and was appointed its supreme adviser in 1983.

Honda received the Order of the Sacred Treasure, First Class, the highest honor bestowed by Japan's emperor. He also received the American auto industry's highest award when he was admitted to the Automobile Hall of Fame in 1989. He was awarded the Automobile Manufacturer Association's highest honor, the Dud Perkins Award in 1971.

Soichiro Honda died in 1991. His passion for bikes, his innovative ideas and willingness to take risks made the Honda Motor Company one of the most respected motorcycle and automobile manufacturers in the world.

Marcus Loew

BIRTH NAME Marcus Loew

BORN May 7, 1870

DIED September 5, 1927

DROPPED OUT Elementary School

FOUNDER OF LOEWS Theatres and the famous Metro-Goldwyn-Mayer (MGM) studios, Marcus Loew was a key-figure behind the success of the American motion picture industry.

Marcus Loew was born in New York City into a family of Austrian immigrants. His mother was Ida Sichel. His father, Herman Loew, worked as a waiter. When Marcus was nine, he left school to help support his large family. He started as a newspaper boy and later took up various odd jobs, learning business skills along the way. He worked in a map-making plant, a garment shop and later in a fur factory. Marcus always dreamed of owning property and becoming a landlord.

In 1904, with the money he had saved doing various small jobs, Loew and Adolph Zukor, another immigrant as well as a fellow dropout, opened a nickelodeon in a rented store. They made enough money that Loew was able to start buying movie houses.

In 1912, Loew started Loew's Theatrical Enterprise. He bought the Metro Pictures Corporation in the early 1920s. Soon he purchased the Goldwyn Picture Corporation, which had run into financial problems. With Louis B. Mayer and Samuel Goldwyn, he formed the Metro-Goldwyn-Mayer (MGM) studio. By 1924, he had 100 theatres and by 1927, he had 144. These were deluxe, modern theatre houses that offered the best entertainment to movie and theatre enthusiasts.

In 1927, before he could see the 24 new movie houses that he had started to build, he died at the age of 57. MGM and Loew's Theatrical Enterprise, however, went on to play a major role in the American movie industry.

In 1954, when the Department of Justice ruled that theatre chains must divest themselves of studios, Loew's Theatrical Enterprise and MGM became separate entities. MGM studios went on to become the largest Hollywood film production studio, responsible for bringing out classics such as *Gone with the Wind* and *The Wizard of Oz*.

Loews Theatres merged with Cineplex Odeon Corporation in 1998 to form Loews Cineplex Entertainment, which operates in major cities across the U.S., Canada and Europe.

Driven by ambition and his love for theatre, Marcus Loew became a successful businessman, responsible for America's largest theatre chain and its biggest studio.

Joseph Pulitzer

BIRTH NAME Joseph Pulitzer
BORN April 10, 1847
DIED October 29, 1911
DROPPED OUT High School

BORN IN MAKÓ, Hungary, Joseph Pulitzer was the eldest son of a grain merchant who died when Joseph was 11. His mother later married a businessman, and Joseph was educated in private schools in Budapest. At 17, he left Hungary and reached the U.S. without a penny in his pocket. Pulitzer was anxious to serve in the military, but both the Austrian Army and the French Foreign Legion had rejected him because of his frail health. He was able to serve in the Union army during the American Civil War. Pulitzer was fluent in Hungarian, German and French, but his English was not perfect. After the war, he settled in St. Louis, first working as a waiter before taking a reporting job with a German-language newspaper, the *Westliche Post*.

Pulitzer had good reporting skills. He succeeded in his work and soon bought the *Post* for $3,000, followed by the *St. Louis Dispatch* for $2,700 dollars, merging the two papers to form the *St. Louis Post-Dispatch*. He took an active part in politics and was elected to the Missouri Legislature. In 1877, he married Kate Davis.

In 1883, Pulitzer bought the New York *World* from Jay Gould. It had been losing $40,000 a year. Pulitzer increased circulation dramatically, with human-interest stories and a crusade against business monopolies. The *World* became the largest newspaper in the U.S., with a circulation of over 600,000.

Pulitzer was elected to Congress from New York in 1885, but he resigned after a few months, deciding he preferred his career in journalism. Pulitzer's paper was one of the pioneers of investigative journalism. It also published the first color comic, "The Yellow Kid."

After 1890, partial blindness and failing health prevented him from taking active part in editorial duties but he continued to have financial control over the paper. The *World* got into a major circulation battle with its rival, William Randolph Hearst's *Sun,* famous for yellow journalism.

Pulitzer died aboard his yatch in 1911. In his will, he left $2 million to create the Graduate School of Journalism at Columbia University, which had been a long cherished dream of his. His will also established the Pulitzer Prize, to recognize excellence in the fields of journalism, music, drama and literature.

Joseph Pulitzer transformed journalism forever, with his investigative reporting, sensational stories and crusades against corruption.

$ **Millionaire Dropouts Trivia** $

Titanic, the highest grossing movie of all time, was directed by a dropout (James Cameron); and the two lead actors were dropouts (Leonardo Di Caprio and Kate Winslet).

Sir Frederick Henry Royce

BIRTH NAME Frederick Henry Royce
BORN March 27, 1863
DIED April 22, 1933
DROPPED OUT Elementary School

FREDERICK HENRY ROYCE was a pioneer in the motorcar industry; he created the luxurious Rolls-Royce automobile. Royce went to great lengths in his drive for perfection. His high ideals and attention to detail are followed to this day by his "boys."

Henry Royce was born in 1863 in Alwalton, England; he was nine when his father died. He dropped out of school to help support his family by delivering newspapers and telegrams. Being interested in engineering and electricity, he worked at the Great Northern Locomotive Works and then at the Electric Light and Power Company in London, becoming, at 19, the company's chief engineer at Liverpool.

Using his modest savings of £20 pounds, together with £50 invested by Ernest Claremont, he founded F.H. Royce & Company. The company manufactured simple products like electric doorbell kits, which became a big success and gave them the freedom to focus on manufacturing dynamos, electric motors and cranes. Royce's dedication to quality products was rigorous right from the start, and the company was very successful. Royce renamed the company Royce Limited in 1899 and increased his share in the company.

Soon Royce shifted his focus to making motorcars. He bought a few cars to study their engineering and decided to build two-cylinder, 10 hp cars in 1903. One of the shareholders in his company, Henry Edmunds, introduced Royce to Charles Rolls, who was looking for a replacement for the Panhard automobile. Rolls was impressed with Royce's cars and they agreed to make cars together and sell them under the Rolls-Royce name, with Royce focusing on the engineering and Rolls selling the cars.

By 1906, Royce had developed a 50 hp car, called the Silver Ghost, which established the company's reputation as manufacturers of the best car in the world. The Silver Ghost was the favorite car of royalty, nobility, maharajahs and heads of state. Other legendary cars produced by Rolls-Royce included the Phantom and the Wraith.

Rolls convinced Royce to become a consultant to the army for the manufacture of a swiveling propeller for the airship Gamma. When Rolls died in an airplane accident in 1911, Royce recognized the need for reliable engines for airplanes. His first aeronautical engine, Eagle, built using technology from the Silver Ghost, was being used in World War I by 1916. His other aero engines, Hawk and Falcon, quickly followed.

Royce launched a second generation of engines for airplanes, the Kestral and the Buzzard, by the late 1920s and constantly worked on the engines to increase horsepower. The Merlin was developed for the Royal Air Force Hurricane and Spitfire fighter planes. His famous R engine won the Schneider Trophy for England in 1929.

Royce was awarded the Order of the British Empire after World War I and made a baronet for his contribution to British aviation in 1930. He remained actively involved in his company's engine designs till his death in 1933 at the age of 70.

Henry Royce began with no technical knowledge. But with his dedication, discipline, attitude and perfectionism he became highly respected in the field of automobile and aeronautical engineering. He believed in improving a successful product rather than taking a risk with a new invention. This philosophy of pursuing excellence is observed in Rolls-Royce even today. His motto, "Whatever is rightly done—however humble—is noble," is still followed at the company.

Rick Rubin

BIRTH NAME Frederick Jay Rubin

BORN March 10, 1963

DROPPED OUT New York University

RICK RUBIN IS the co-founder of Def Jam Records, a trend set-ting label for hip-hop, rap and rock music. Rubin's passion in life is music; it is through music that he deciphers everything in the world. Often described as an enigma, he connects with people through his love for music.

Rubin was born on Long Island and grew up listening to the Beatles. Graduating from high school in 1981, he entered New York University and while he was there founded the Def Jam record label with Russell Simmons in 1984. Some of their early releases included bands like LL Cool J, Public Enemy, Beastie Boys and Run DMC. Def Jam's records usually combined rap and heavy rock.

Rubin and Simmons parted ways in 1988, with the latter heading Def Jam in New York and Rubin moving to Los Angeles to start the Def American label. He went on to sign several heavy rock bands, including Slayer, Danzig, Masters of Reality, The Cult and Wolfs-bane. He also signed The Jesus & Mary Chain and the stand-up comedian Andrew Dice Clay.

One of Rubin's most successful ventures was producing the breakthrough album of the Red Hot Chili Peppers, *Blood Sugar Sex Magik*. Rubin had close ties with rap artists also, signing the Geto Boys and carried on working with Public Enemy and LL Cool J. He encouraged collaboration between Aerosmith and Run DMC to produce their trendsetting song *Walk This Way*.

Signaling a new era in his career, Rubin renamed his company American Recordings, removing the word Def, for which he held a symbolic funeral. The first project under the new banner was Johnny Cash's *American Recordings*, in 1994, which was instrumental in re-viving Johnny Cash's flagging career. Rubin also produced records for a number of older artists such as Tom Petty, Donovan and Neil Diamond.

In 2003, Rubin launched Mars Volta, a progressive rock group, with their album *De-Loused in the Comatorium,* giving his company, too, a new direction. In the same year, Rubin made the track *99 Problems* for Jay Z's *The Black Album,* for which he also appeared in the video. He produced Slipknot's hugely successful *Vol. 3 (The Subliminal Verses).* Some of his other projects include System of a Down's *Mezmerize,* with Daron Malakian, Weezer's *Make Believe,* Shakira's *Oral Fixation 1&2* and Audioslave's *Out of Exile.*

It is Rubin's love for music that enables him to recognize good music long before it becomes popular and before actually making the tracks in the recording studio. Not particularly fond of working in the studio, he considers recording a process of bringing to life what is already in his head. He likens it to the notion of sculpture as a process of seeing the work in the block of stone and chipping away all the other parts to reveal the figure. He revels in being a true artist, letting his imagination flow to create unique music.

Rubin was instrumental in the rise of hip-hop music, lending his style of merging rap and heavy metal to several records in the pre-gangsta era. He is famous for always being ahead of the curve and knowing where the music industry is headed.

The recent proliferation of artists and the excessive importance given to producers is something that upsets Rick Rubin. With the competition increasing among artists, the emphasis has shifted from artist to song and from lyrics to promotion. To a music lover like Rubin, this trend is not a positive one, for he believes in the power of words and music, in experimenting with different styles and above all in entertaining people.

Harland Sanders

BIRTH NAME Harland David Sanders
BORN November 9, 1890
DIED December 16, 1980
DROPPED OUT Middle School

HARLAND SANDERS IS the entrepreneur behind the "finger lickin' good" Kentucky Fried Chicken (KFC) chain of fast food restaurants. A pioneer in the fast food business, he combined his love for cooking with his shrewd business acumen to start what is today the world's largest restaurant company.

Harland Sanders was born in Henryville, Indiana. His father Wilbert Sanders was a butcher. When Harland was six, his father died. His mother, Margaret Dunlevy Sanders, was forced to work in a factory, leaving Harland to take care of his three-year-old brother and baby sister. Those were tough days. His mother used to sew at night to make some money. Left to cook at home, Harland soon learned to cook a variety of dishes. By the age of seven, he had almost mastered the art.

When Harland was in sixth grade, he had to drop out of school to work full time. He worked on a farm near his house for two dollars a month to support his family. When he was 12, his mother married a produce farmer and moved to suburban Indianapolis. Harland left for a job on a farm in Greenwood, Indiana. At 15, he worked as a streetcar conductor. At 16, he was a private in Cuba. He took up various odd jobs, working as a steamboat ferry operator, firefighter and insurance salesman. He sold tires and operated a service station.

When he was 40, Sanders started making chicken for people who passed by his service station in Corbin, Kentucky. He had no restaurant and no tables either, but he served his customers on a dining table in his own living quarters. His new business attracted crowds and he soon moved to a restaurant across the street. He developed his blend of 11 herbs and spices that are used today to season chicken at KFC restaurants worldwide. He perfected his technique of using a pressure cooker instead of pan-frying, thus reducing the cooking time. In recognition of his contribution to the state's cuisine, Governor Ruby Laffoon made him a Kentucky Colonel in 1935.

In the early 1950s, Colonel Sanders closed his business when Interstate 75 bypassed Corbin. Living on $105 a month in Social Security payments, he traveled by car across the country developing his franchise business. He got a nickel for each chicken sold in those restaurants. By 1964, he had over 600 chicken outlets in the U.S. and Canada. His became one of the most recognizable faces in the U.S.

He later sold the company for $2 million to a group of investors. The company went public in 1966 and was listed on the New York Stock Exchange in 1969. Heublein Inc. acquired it in 1971 for $285 million. In 1986, it was sold to R. J. Reynolds, who again sold it to PepsiCo for $840 million. KFC, Taco Bell and Pizza Hut were all brought under Tricon Global Restaurants Inc. by PepsiCo, which later sought shareholders' approval to change the name to Yum! Brands. The company now owns A&W All-American Food Restaurants, KFC, Long John Silvers, Pizza Hut and Taco Bell restaurants. It is the world's largest restaurant company.

Colonel Harland Sanders died in 1980 at the age of 90. His passion for cooking and his ability to fight the odds made him a successful entrepreneur.

David Sarnoff

BIRTH NAME David Sarnoff

BORN February 27, 1891

DIED December 12, 1971

DROPPED OUT High School

A VISIONARY WHO foresaw the huge potential of radio and television broadcasting, David Sarnoff led the Radio Corporation of America (RCA) from 1919 to 1970.

David Sarnoff was born in Uzlian, Russia. His father Abraham Leah Sarnoff was a painter. When David was five, his father moved to the U.S. to earn more money. David was sent to his great uncle's home to study the Talmud, the compilation of Jewish teachings. He led a disciplined life memorizing the sacred text.

In 1900, Abraham Sarnoff moved the whole family to the U.S. David learned that his father's health was failing and that his father was working very hard to make a living. David was only nine at the time, but he decided to work to support his family.

He began selling Yiddish-language newspapers in New York City, picking up bundles of newspaper as early as 4 AM in order to beat the competition from other delivery boys. He also earned some extra income singing in his synagogue. As he had very little time to study, he started taking English classes at the Educational Alliance. He learned enough English to read the newspaper and learned some business skills as well. He set up a newspaper stand when he was 14. He could not continue in high school as he had to work full-time to take care of his family.

Sarnoff got a job as an office boy for the Marconi Wireless Telegraph Company, becoming a junior operator in 1908. He advanced quickly in the company, always finding a way to be at the right place at the right time to meet and impress the people who could advance his career, including Marconi himself on his visits to the New York office.

Sarnoff moved quickly up the ladder at Marconi. In 1915, he suggested that the company develop a radio music box. His dream was to bring music to the homes of America. With World War I in progress, his plans were put on hold. After the war, Marconi's U.S. assets were absorbed into General Electric and the Radio Corporation of America (RCA) was spun off.

Sarnoff promoted the idea of creating broadcast programming to give people a reason to buy radio receivers. The Jack Dempsey–Georges Carpentier prizefight was the first special event broadcast. Radio sales soared and in three years, though a radio cost $75, sales reached $83.5 million. Sarnoff's next move was to create a national network for broadcasting. In 1926, as the general manager of RCA, he started the National Broadcasting Company (NBC). He was eager to introduce television as well, hoping to supply "sight with sound." Sarnoff predicted that television would become an important factor in America's economy. In 1939, at the New York World Fair, television was introduced. World War II hampered the growth of television; but, after the war, RCA introduced television in a big way and eventually RCA set color TV standards for all American broadcasters.

David Sarnoff retired in 1970 and died a year later in his sleep. With his keen foresight and great determination, he brought about a revolution in the broadcasting industry.

Vidal Sassoon

BIRTH NAME Vidal Sassoon

BORN January 17, 1928

DROPPED OUT Elementary School

VIDAL SASSOON'S CHAIN of hair salons is known worldwide for its wide range of hair products and chic hairstyles. In the mid-1960s, he created hairstyles like the wash-and-wear perm and the hugely popular classic bob cut.

Sassoon was born in the East End of London and had a tough childhood. Vidal's father left home when he was five; he and his little brother spent six years in an orphanage. The family was reunited only after his mother married again and took her children with her.

When Sassoon was 14, his mother had a dream in which she saw him in a barbershop. Although he wanted to be a football player, his mother felt that he should seek a profession in order to earn some money. She took him to Adolph Cohen's Beauty and Barber Shop in the East End, where he began his initial training. He decided that if he had to become a hairstylist, he might as well become the best in the industry.

Sassoon soon realized that his cockney accent was taking him nowhere. He wanted to join the stylish and posh West End salons, but realized that he had to learn to speak proper English in order to do that. He started going to the theatre in the evenings to learn proper English. He spent a lot of time listening and voice training.

Influenced by his mother, who was politically active and had joined the anti-Fascist movement, Sassoon took an active part in the movement. Putting his career on hold in 1948, he left London to join Israel's War of Independence. He wanted to stay on, attend the university and become an architect but was forced to return to London because his family was poor and needed his support.

In 1960, Sassoon returned to London and opened a salon on Bond Street in Mayfair. He worked hard and perfected new techniques to get simple and elegant styles. He soon became famous for his innovative cuts and began to be known as the "founder of modern hairdressing."

His method of haircutting became popularly known as "Sassooning"; models, film stars and other celebrities started sporting his hairstyles. The 60s in Britain was a time of creativity. Sassoon's association with fashion designer Mary Quant made him even more popular. His $5,000 haircut to create an elfin look for Mia Farrow on the sets of the horror film Rosemary's Baby made headlines everywhere.

Sassoon has authored two bestselling books and has hosted his own TV show. Many successful hairstylists have trained in his schools and he has a huge range of hair care products that are known worldwide.

Although Vidal Sassoon could not attend regular school and had to drop out early in order to earn a living, his determination to be the best helped him leave a lasting impression in the world of fashion.

$ **Millionaire Dropouts Trivia** $

**Four out of five of America's richest people
are dropouts:
number 1, Bill Gates, worth $50 billion;
number 3, Paul Allen, worth $22 billion;
number 4, Michael Dell, worth $17.1 billion;
number 5, Sheldon Adelson, worth $6.1 billion.**

Dave Thomas

BIRTH NAME David Thomas

BORN February 7, 1932

DIED January 8, 2002

DROPPED OUT High School

D AVE THOMAS WAS a pioneer in the restaurant business. He founded the Wendy's Old Fashioned Hamburgers chain.

Dave Thomas was born in Atlantic City, New Jersey, to a single mother. When he was only six weeks old, he was adopted by Rex and Auleva Thomas. He was barely five years old when Auleva Thomas died of rheumatic fever and young Dave Thomas spent his childhood years moving from place to place as his adoptive father Rex went looking for jobs. A memorable part of Dave's childhood was the time he spent with his grandmother in Michigan. Dave's emphasis on respect for people and maintaining excellent quality of service were values he learned from her.

Thomas started working at 12, as a counterman at a restaurant in Knoxville. He loved the restaurant business so much that he always dreamt of opening a hamburger restaurant. When he was 15, he dropped out of school and worked at the Hobby House Restaurant in Ft. Wayne. It was here that he met Colonel Sanders, founder of Kentucky Fried Chicken, who was a major source of inspiration and influence in his life. He helped restore four KFC units that were not doing well and sold them back to KFC, becoming a millionaire at 35.

In 1969, Thomas's dream to open a restaurant of his own came true when he started the Wendy's Old Fashioned Hamburger restaurant in Columbus, Ohio, naming the chain after his young daughter. He wanted the restaurant to be a place where families could enjoy made-to-order, hot-off-the-grill sandwiches and fresh beef hamburgers that are square rather than round. He always said, "At Wendy's we don't cut corners!" The restaurant became such a success that Thomas received a number of awards and honors. He became a pioneer in the fast food industry and a role model for managers in the restaurant business.

Adoption was an issue that was very close to Dave's heart, having been an adopted child himself. He wanted to see that every child had a permanent home. When he was asked to head the White House Initiative on Adoption in 1990, he found that there were many obstacles to adoption. In 1992, he started the Dave Thomas Foundation for Adoption, a not-for-profit organization. His initiative helped in the passing of two bills—a one-time tax credit of $5,000 for adoptive parents, and the Adoption and Safe Families Act. The two bills helped in making the adoption process easier and more affordable. The foundation also worked with the U.S. Postal Service to bring out a colorful 33-cent adoption postage stamp that said, "Adopting a Child, Shaping a Life, Building a Home, Creating a World."

Thomas funded the Gordon Teter Chair for Pediatric Cancer Research, the Dave Thomas Family Primary Care Center and The Dave and Lorraine Thomas Clinical Laboratory at the Children's Hospital in Columbus. He established a number of educational centers and programs. Always haunted by the fact that he had dropped out of school, he went back to school 45 years later and got his GED from Coconut Creek High School in Ft Lauderdale. He considered this one of his greatest achievements. Although he was an extraordinarily successful businessman, he considered his family—his wife Lorraine, his five children and 16 grandchildren—his biggest accomplishment.

The Wendy's TV commercials with Thomas as the Wendy's spokesman, made him the most recognizable face in America; and people loved him for his down-to-earth, simple style. The campaign made it into the *Guinness Book of World Records* as the longest running television advertising campaign starring a company founder.

When Thomas died in 2002, at 69, from cancer of the liver, he had become an American folk hero who used his heart and his millions to create a better world.

Kemmons Wilson

BIRTH NAME Charles Kemmons Wilson
BORN January 5, 1913
DIED February 12, 2003
DROPPED OUT High School

K EMMONS WILSON FOUNDED the Holiday Inn hotel chain. He started out with the dream of providing tourists comfortable, clean and affordable lodging. He ended up revolutionizing the lodging industry worldwide.

Kemmons Wilson was born in Osceola, Arkansas. His father was an insurance salesman who died when Kemmons was nine months old. His mother, Ruby "Doll" Wilson, moved to Memphis, Tennessee, where she got a job as a dental assistant. Kemmons grew up in Memphis under her guidance. When he was 14, he was delivering a bicycle to a store when a car hit him. It was believed at that time that he could never walk again, but he recovered with the help of his doctor, Willis Campbell.

When Wilson's mother lost her job during the Great Depression, he was forced to drop out of school and look for a job. With a loan of $50 from a friend, he set up a popcorn machine in a theatre lobby. In 1933, he bought a house for himself and his mother with the money he made. His mother drilled into his head that he could do anything he wanted to do and Wilson firmly believed that.

In 1951, Wilson was on vacation with his wife, his two sons and three daughters, when he was forced to pay two dollars extra for each child in a motel. He thought it unfair that the motels charged so much and did not even provide enough comforts for what they charged.

Wilson felt the traveling public deserved better and vowed to start a chain of motels that would provide clean, comfortable and affordable accommodation to tourists. His wife did not take him seriously at the time, but Wilson made notes, measured the rooms and came back to Memphis with enough information to start on his plan. Adopting the name Holiday Inn from an old Bing Crosby movie that his draftsman had seen, Wilson sketched out his design. The first Holiday Inn opened in August 1952. He made sure that his motels had air-conditioning, swimming pool and restaurant facilities. Most of all, he ensured that children were not charged extra. Holiday Inn went International in 1960. Today, there are many Holiday Inns across the U.S. and many more in other countries as well.

Wilson received a number of awards and honors. He it was inducted into the American Motel Magazine Hall of Fame in 1961; and he received the Golden Plate Award in 1965, the Horatio Alger Award in 1970 and the Northwood University Outstanding Business Leader Award in 1985. He was inducted into the International Franchise Association Hall of Fame in 1989. He has also received five honorary degrees.

In his autobiography, *Half Luck and Half Brains,* he shares his experience of how a high school dropout could become a successful entrepreneur. He died in Memphis in 2003.

Driven by self-belief and ambition, Kemmons Wilson achieved what he wanted to. He demonstrated to the world that if one is hard working and determined, nothing can come in the way of success.

$ **Millionaire Dropouts Trivia** $

Dropouts include:
- **22 Knights**
- **10 Nobel laureates**
- **4 Pulitzer prize winners**
- **6 Olympic gold medal winners**
- **Winners of 84 Academy Awards**
- **13 Presidents of the United States**
- **30 Additional Academy Award nominees**
- **19 members of the Rock and Roll Hall of Fame**
- **11 members of the Country Music Hall of Fame**

Millionaire Dropouts Trivia

Many of the world's greatest inventions were developed by dropouts, including television, radio, airplanes, cars, motion pictures, the incandescent light bulb, the car stereo tape deck, the gas mask, the traffic signal, earmuffs, the game of basketball, the sewing machine—and many more.

Inventors

Inventors

Inventors

Inventors

Inventors

Inventors

Inventors

Inventors

Inventors

Thomas Edison

BIRTH NAME Thomas Alva Edison
BORN February 11, 1847
DIED October 18, 1931
DROPPED OUT Elementary School

THOMAS ALVA EDISON was born in Milan, Ohio, the youngest of Samuel and Nancy Edison's seven children. The family moved to Port Huron, Michigan when Al, as he was then called, was seven. He got a late start in school, and the three months he spent in the educational system did not go well, with his teacher describing him as "addled." His mother, being a teacher herself, decided to school him at home. Al learned most of his lessons from the R.G. Parker's book, School of Natural Philosophy.

At 13, Edison started selling newspapers and candy on a train, setting up a lab and a printing press in a baggage car and publishing the first newspaper ever printed on a train. When he was 16, he saved a little boy named Jimmie from being hit by a runaway railcar. Jimmie's father was so grateful that he took Edison under his wing and trained him to be a telegraph operator. Edison was partially deaf and hence not easily distracted by the operator next to him or other outside noise.

The rapid expansion of the telegraph industry in the late nineteenth century offered a number of opportunities and Edison traveled from place to place within the United States in the years 1863–1868, taking telegraph jobs and continuing his experiments. He ended in Boston in 1868, working for Western Union and working on his inventions. He quit at the beginning of 1869, at 22, to become a full-time inventor. He patented an electric vote recorder, a commercial failure; and Edison resolved that he would invent only things that people found useful. In 1869, he moved to New York and continued experimenting with telegraphy, inventing, among other things, the Universal

Stock Printer, the first electricity-based broadcast system. With the $40,000 he earned for this and related inventions, he set up a small laboratory in Newark, New Jersey. In 1876, he set up his research laboratory in Menlo Park, New Jersey, where his staff could work on many inventions at once. This was really the first laboratory devoted to research and development of practical products, and the lab itself may be Edison's greatest invention. While he continued to experiment, his primary role was in supervising and directing the work of others, many of them better trained and more scientifically inclined than Edison himself.

In 1877, Edison invented his first phonograph. Sound was recorded on tin foil cylinders in the machine and then reproduced. He toured the country promoting the device for use as a dictation machine and was invited to the White House to show the device to President Rutherford B. Hayes in 1878. It would be nearly a decade later before Edison took an interest in recorded music discs for home entertainment.

The bulk of Edison's patents, whether they pertained to the telegraph, the telephone or the electric light, were for improvements to technologies others had invented. Edison, though, did invent the first motion picture camera, along with a system to view the films.

Edison greatly improved the light bulb after purchasing the patent from Henry Woodward and Mathew Evans. He applied his trial-and-error process to finding a long-lasting filament material and went on to manufacture light bulbs and demonstrate them in cities around the world. He became one of the pioneers of the electrical generation and transmission industry.

Thomas Alva Edison, "the wizard of Menlo Park," as one newspaper reporter dubbed him, is the world's most famous inventor of all time. February 11, Edison's birthday, is celebrated as National Inventors' Day in America. With his technological and organizational innovations, Thomas Alva Edison proved his teacher wrong and revolutionized the way we live in this world.

Florence Melton

BIRTH NAME Florence Spurgeon

BORN November 6, 1911

DROPPED OUT Elementary School

BORN IN PHILADELPHIA, Florence Spurgeon grew up in a family that stressed the importance of charity not just for recognition, but as a means of rendering genuine help to mankind. Florence was greatly influenced by her grandmother, who taught her Jewish values and inspired her to be a loving and caring human being.

Soon after moving to Columbus, Ohio, in the early 1940s, Florence, now married to Aaron Zacks, served on the Board of United Way and the Red Cross Nutrition Corps. She also served on the board of the Huntington National Bank, becoming the first woman to do so; and she was a founding member of the Coalition for the Advancement of Jewish Education (CAJE).

On a trip to visit the Firestone Tire and Rubber Company in Akron, in 1947, Mrs. Zacks saw a piece of foam latex, a material Firestone had developed during World War II. The company was searching for ideas to use the material. Mrs. Zacks came up with the idea of making a slipper out of it. She stitched up a soft, washable, foam-soled slipper and quickly sold a lot of them.

Later that same year, Mrs. Zacks, her husband and a partner started the R.G. Barry Corporation to manufacture the new Angel Treads Slippers. R.G. Barry became the largest manufacturer of comfort footwear in the world.

After her first husband's death, Mrs. Zacks married industrialist and philanthropist Samuel M Melton in 1968. With his support, she launched a novel method to promote Jewish education. Always having been passionate about it, she started the Florence Melton Adult Mini-School, together with her husband and the Hebrew University of Jerusalem.

The school offers a two-year program and introduces adult learners to the complexity, depth and beauty of the Jewish heritage. Mrs. Melton has been actively involved in the Mini-School, first as chairperson of the board and later as chairperson emerita. With her guidance, the school has evolved and begun to grow in new directions. These adult mini-schools have over 6,000 students, 17,000 alumni and a faculty of over 300 in more than 60 cities across the globe.

Mrs. Melton's passion for Jewish education has been such that she has served on various committees and commissions both locally and internationally. In recognition of her good work, she has been given numerous honorary degrees and awards.

Mrs. Melton has a creative side to her, too, writing poetry, plays and music; and in 1994, at 82, she became a Bat Mitzvah at Congregation Tifereth Israel.

Florence Melton has not merely been a successful entrepreneur and innovator. Her dedication and sense of service has made her a truly successful human being as well.

$ **Millionaire Dropouts Trivia** $

**A member of the all-time top selling band
The Beatles, George Harrison, was a dropout.**

Earl Muntz

BIRTH NAME Earl Muntz

BORN 1914(?)

DIED June 20, 1987

DROPPED OUT High School

EARL MUNTZ WAS born in Elgin, Illinois. As a small boy he loved playing with gadgets. He built his own radio at 8 and one of the first car radios at 14. He started selling used cars when he was 20; his mother had to sign all the paperwork, as he wasn't old enough.

In 1941, Muntz moved to Glendale, California, and opened a used car lot, followed by another in Los Angeles. He signed up adman Mike Shore, who devised gimmicks that made Muntz the largest used car seller in the country. They pitched "Madman Muntz," and his crazy prices, but Muntz was crazy as a fox, buying used cars in the Midwest, paying servicemen $50 apiece to drive the cars west, and selling the cars for twice what he paid.

Muntz went from selling cars cheap to selling cheap TVs. He was a high school dropout, but he had more common sense than the engineers he hired to design televisions. His cost-cutting technique—snipping out one component after another with the wire cutters he carried in his shirt pocket until a circuit quit working, then telling the engineer to add back that one component—became known as "muntzing." His barebones circuitry made for a television that only worked well in urban areas with a strong broadcast signal; but that's where the market was and he was able to compete with the major brands. He was able to get televisions down below $200 retail for the first time and eventually produced a model that broke the $100 barrier, selling for $99.95. He promoted his low-cost sets with heavy advertising, including skywriting over major cities. It was Muntz's skywriting—paid for by the letter—that resulted in the abbreviation *TV* for *television*.

Muntz leveraged his nationwide reputation to introduce the first American-built sports car, the Muntz Jet. He bought the design rights to an aluminum-body two-seat sports car initially developed by an Indy 500 race car designer, Frank Kurtis. Kurtis had built fewer than 20 cars and was no marketer. Muntz added a rear seat on a longer wheelbase, replaced the aluminum sheet metal with steel, put in a bigger engine, and proceeded to lose a thousand dollars on every car he sold. It was the only business he started that never made money. Today the cars, of which fewer than 500 were built, are collector's items worth more than 10 times their original selling price of $5,500.

The advent of color television forced Muntz's cheap black and white sets off the market, and Muntz went bankrupt, losing millions. But he went on to apply his particular brand of innovation to automotive sound systems, harking back to his tinkering as a boy. He invented the four-track car stereo, precursor to the eight-track system that would become a standard car accessory for two decades. He licensed music from the major record labels and sold four-track tapes for his installed base.

Muntz kept going from business to business until his death in 1987, at 73. Earl Muntz's passion for machines and new technology, combined with his innovative marketing strategy made him one of the best known and most successful inventors and retailers of his time.

Isaac Merrit Singer

BIRTH NAME Isaac Merrit Singer

BORN October 27, 1811

DIED July 23, 1875

DROPPED OUT Middle School

ISAAC MERRIT SINGER was born near Pittstown, New York. When he was 10, his parents divorced. His father remarried, and Isaac didn't get along with his stepmother. When he was 12, he moved to Oswego, New York, to stay with his older brother, working in his brother's machine shop as an apprentice.

When he was 19, Singer worked for a few months as a machinist but left to join a touring troupe of actors. The same year, he married for the first time and settled in New York City for a few years before returning to upstate New York, this time in the Cooperstown area, to work in another machine shop.

Singer continued to alternate among being a machinist, being an actor, and being a groom (not always remembering to get divorced first). He received his first patent in 1839, for a rock-drilling machine. He sold the patent for $2,000 and used the money to form the Merritt Players. After five years, the troupe disbanded because of financial losses, and Singer took a job in a print shop in Fredericksburg, Ohio, where the troupe was when it broke up. There he came up with an idea for a machine to cut wood blocks used in printing. He moved to Pittsburgh and then back to New York City, where he built a prototype of the machine. When that prototype was destroyed in a boiler explosion, a machinist who had heard about the machine, Orson Phelps, invited Singer to Boston to recreate it

Working in the Phelps shop, where the wood cutting machine eventually turned out to be unsuccessful, Singer took a look at some Lerow and Blodgett sewing machines. He quickly found a way to improve them, making them much more reliable, easier to manufacture and easier to use. He received a patent for his improved design in 1851, at 40.

Forming a partnership with George B Zieber and Phelps, Singer founded the Jenny Lind Sewing Machine Company, later changing the name to I.M. Singer & Co. Elias Howe had developed and patented a sewing machine in 1846; he and several other sewing machine manufacturers separately entered into a series of legal battles with Singer. These were resolved by the manufacturers agreeing to pool their patents instead of fighting in court. This agreement became the first patent pool that allowed production of complicated machines without legal battles over patent rights.

By late 1860s, Singer became the world's largest producer of sewing machines and Isaac Singer became a wealthy man. Singer's machines were designed for both domestic and commercial use. They were reliable, long lasting and, thanks to Singer's introduction of the installment credit plans, affordable.

In 1867, Singer established a factory in Scotland at Clydebank, near Glasgow, entering the European market. He later set up factories in Paris and Rio de Janeiro, making Singer the first American-based multinational corporation.

After Singer's death in 1875, his many children and many wives fought over his two wills to divide his estate of about $14,000,000 among them.

Isaac Merit Singer used his creative energy to develop the world's first practical sewing machine and to start the first multinational company based in the United States.

Wilbur & Orville Wright

BIRTH NAMES Wilbur Wright, Orville Wright
WILBUR: BORN April 16, 1867
DIED May 30, 1912
ORVILLE: BORN August 19, 1871
DIED January 30, 1948
DROPPED OUT High School

WILBUR WRIGHT WAS born in Millville, Indiana. Four years later, his brother Orville was born in Dayton, Ohio. Their father, Milton Wright was a minister in the Church of the United Brethren in Christ. The boys had a good childhood. Their father often bought them toys and other trinkets; When they were 7 and 11, he brought home a small flying toy that inspired their interest in flying. Some years later, the boys tried to build something similar to it. Calling their models "bats," they discovered that the larger they were, the less they flew. When all attempts to make them fly failed, Orville and Wilbur returned to kite flying.

Wilbur was a good student and would have graduated from high school, had the family not moved during his senior year. Orville was only an average student and dropped out of school to start a printing company with his brother. Always tinkering with gadgets, the boys started repairing their friends' bicycles. In 1893, they set up a bicycle repair shop of their own and later went on to make and sell their own bicycles.

In 1896 the Wrights' interest in flying was rekindled when they read of the death of a French experimenter. They studied the available literature and engineering calculations related to both powered flight and gliding—or soaring—flight. Their interest was more in the latter, as it presented interesting questions, they thought, relating to control of the flight path.

The Wright brothers carefully and methodically analyzed the problem of flight: managing propulsion, lift, and control, the last of which had largely been ignored by others. They checked and corrected published calculations. They built a wind tunnel and conducted hundreds of experiments with models. They built ever-larger gliders, experimenting with them at Kitty Hawk each year to be sure they understood how flight control worked before they attempted powered flight. Their major breakthrough, on top of all their other improvements, was understanding how to control the direction of flight by changing the shape of the wing. They accomplished this, with their lightweight wood and fabric wings, by physically bending the wing, using cables attached to levers. Today's giant passenger jets use flaps to accomplish the same thing.

In 1903 they returned to Kitty Hawk with a powered plane. They had designed and fabricated a propeller and engine, with a bicycle chain drive, of course. On December 17, at 10:35 AM, with Orville Wright at the controls, the first controlled, machine-powered, sustained flight took off; it lasted 12 seconds.

The Wrights continued to develop their design, using methods that would be familiar to any modern engineer, and obtained a patent for the Wright Flying Machine in 1906. Their planes became the world's first military airplanes and the two brothers impressed the whole world after successful demonstrations and exhibitions in France, Italy, Germany and the United States.

Neither brother ever married, their only passion being aviation. Wilbur Wright died at the age of 45 from typhoid. In 1932, a national monument was dedicated to the Wright brothers at Kitty Hawk. In 1948, at the age of 77, Orville Wright died of heart attack.

The Wright brothers' hard work and their passion for flying gave the world its first practical airplane and opened the skies for everyone.

Millionaire Dropouts Trivia

America's richest elementary school dropout, the late H.L. Hunt, was worth billions.

Powerful Dropouts

Powerful Dropouts

Powerful Dropouts

Powerful Dropouts

Powerful Dropouts

Powerful Dropouts

Powerful Dropouts

Powerful Dropouts

Powerful Dropouts

Mortimer J. Adler

BIRTH NAME Mortimer Jerome Adler

BORN December 28, 1902

DIED June 28, 2001

DROPPED OUT High School

MORTIMER J. ADLER was an education theorist, author and philosopher who advocated the study of philosophy for everyone and the need to apply it in every sphere of daily life. He is often considered a zealot for his single-minded pursuit of making the classics the basis of all education.

Adler was born in New York City, where his father was a jewelry salesman and his mother was a schoolteacher. He dropped out of high school at 14 to focus on his job as a copyboy at *The New York Sun*. Mortimer decided to take night classes at Columbia University to become a journalist. It was in these classes that he first read John Stuart Mill and became fascinated with philosophy. He resolved to read Plato and other philosophers to further his knowledge.

Adler received a scholarship from Columbia University for his undergraduate studies but was not awarded a degree, as he did not complete his physical education course, which he declared to be "a nuisance." He then joined the graduate program and impressed the faculty to such an extent that he was invited to join as staff while he was only a student. Adler received a Ph.D. even though he never got his undergraduate degree.

Adler became an advocate for the integration of science, literature and philosophy, stressing the need for philosophy to be practical more than theoretical. He wanted young people to gain knowledge through discussions and debates. He compiled a book, *Dialectic*, in 1927, in which he summarized the major philosophical and religious ideas of the western world. In 1952, Adler and Robert M. Hutchins edited *Great Books of the Western World*, a 54-volume set published by Encyclopedia Britannica.

Adler's other important publications with Britannica were *Gateway to the Great Books*, *The Great Ideas Program* and *The Annals of America*. In the *Propaedia* he outlined all human knowledge. Adler taught first at Columbia University, then at the University of Chicago and later at the University of North Carolina. He also was on the board at Britannica and at The Ford Foundation.

Adler co-founded the Institute for Philosophical Research at the University of North Carolina, The Aspen Institute and The Center for the Study of The Great Ideas.

The works of Aristotle and St. Thomas Aquinas influenced Adler deeply. He believed in a liberal course of study with philosophy and arts as the basis of education. He thought students should not have to select vocational courses. He recognized the importance of education for three key reasons; to learn how to spend leisure time, how to make a living ethically and how to be a responsible citizen.

Adler tried to bring philosophy to the masses, so they could delve into a subject rather than just know it superficially. He strove to make his writing accessible to any reader, not just academics. Two of his most famous and influential books are *How to Read a Book* and *How to Think About War and Peace*.

Mortimer Adler died in June 2001 after successfully sowing the seed of philosophical interest in the minds of millions of young Americans. The world will remember him for his emphasis on making philosophy the foundation of all educational reform.

Jane Austen

BIRTH NAME Jane Austen

BORN December 16, 1775

DIED July 18, 1817

DROPPED OUT Abbey School

JANE AUSTEN, THE prominent English novelist who wrote the classics *Pride and Prejudice, Emma* and *Mansfield Park,* was born in Steventon, Hampshire, in 1775, to Rev. George Austen and Cassandra Leigh. She was the youngest of seven children. Her father was the rector in Steventon and Jane spent her first sixteen years there. Jane's father retired in 1801 and moved his family to Bath, where he died four years later. Jane never married and lived with her mother and beloved sister Cassandra, who also remained single. They moved first to Southampton in 1805, then to Chawton in 1809, living in a house on their brother Edward's estate until Jane died in 1817.

Austen was educated at home for a short time by a relative and from 1785 to 1786 at the Abbey boarding school in Reading, Berkshire, receiving a better education than what was usually accorded to girls in her time. Austen started writing novels in 1798; but before that, as a child, she wrote many short plays for the amusement of her family.

Austen was engaged to be married, for less than a day, to Harris Bigg-Wither, in December 1802. Apart from this event, she led a peaceful and quiet life among the local provincial society, where she used her keen observations of human relationships and behavior in her writings.

Initially, publishers did not take her writings seriously. Some works lay forgotten with them for almost ten years and, when finally published, were not in the same order as she had written them. Her most famous work was *Pride and Prejudice,* written in 1796–97, but published in 1813. Austen's first novel, *Northanger Abbey,* was published posthumously. It is believed that the character of Catherine Morland in the novel was based on her own childhood.

Austen wrote *Sense and Sensibility* under the title *Eleanor and Marianne*, in 1797–98. Between then and 1809, she only wrote *The Watson*. From 1809 on, she revised all her early works for publication. Three of her later works, written between 1811 and 1816, were *Mansfield Park*, *Emma* and *Persuasion*. *Mansfield Park* and *Emma* are considered among her best works, with great depth and subtlety in the portrayal of their characters.

Austen's initial works were published anonymously. Sense and Sensibility was published in 1811 as authored "By a Lady." With its success, Austen started to revise First Impressions, later renamed *Pride and Prejudice. Mansfield Park* was published in 1814 and sold out in six months. Her next novel, *Emma,* was published in 1815 and dedicated to the Prince Regent. Austen started on *Persuasion* in 1815 and completed it in 1816, when she became ill. She started her next novel, *Sandition,* in 1817 but was not able to complete it and moved to Winchester to be treated. She died there in 1817, supposedly of Addison's disease, and was buried in Winchester Cathedral.

Austen's strength was in her depiction of finely defined characters, using ordinary and everyday settings. She highlighted their eccentricities in behavior and emotion, letting the readers discover interesting facets of their personalities, without dispensing any moral lessons. Her novels revolved around women and she featured them in almost every scene, evidently because she did not know how men behaved when not in their presence.

Critics agree that no other author has been able to portray the trivialities of daily life in small provincial towns as well as Jane Austen. She is easily the most celebrated novelist of her period in English literature.

Dame Agatha Christie

BIRTH NAME: Agatha Mary Clarissa Miller

BORN: September 15, 1890

DIED: January 12, 1976

DROPPED OUT: Home-schooled

AGATHA CHRISTIE IS the world's most eminent writer of mystery novels and short stories. She is famous for creating the characters Hercule Poirot and Miss Marple and has sold more than a billion books.

Agatha was born in Torquay, in Devon, in 1890. Her father, Frederick Alvah Miller, was an American with a modest private income; but he died when she was a child. Her mother, Clarissa, decided to educate her at home and urged her to write from the time she was young. When she was sixteen, she went to school in Paris to study piano and singing. Agatha became an accomplished pianist but did not pursue a musical career, as she was shy and could not overcome stage fright. After a trip to Cairo with her mother, she wrote her first novel and started writing short stories.

She married Colonel Archibald Christie, an officer of the Royal Flying Corp, in 1914. A daughter, Rosalind was born in 1919. The marriage was not a happy one and ended in 1926 when she learned that her husband had fallen in love with a younger woman named Nancy Neele. The same year her adored mother died, prompting her to disappear for eleven days and live in a hotel in Harrowgate under the name of Mrs. Neele. She later claimed to have suffered amnesia and a nervous breakdown due to stress. This incident was later recounted in the movie Agatha, starring Vanessa Redgrave, in 1979.

Christie was married for the second time in 1930, to Sir Max Mallowan, whom she had met in 1927 on her travels to the Near East. Sir Max was a renowned British archeologist and was 14 years younger than Christie. Several of her novels, including *Death on the*

Nile and *Murder in Mesopotamia,* were based on her travels with him to Syria and Iraq.

Christie worked at a Red Cross hospital in Torquay as a dispenser and worked at a pharmacy during World War I. This work influenced her writing, as it gave her detailed knowledge of poisons. Several of her books involve murders conducted using poison.

In her first detective novel, *The Mysterious Affair at Styles,* Christie introduced the Belgian detective Hercule Poirot. The character was well received and appeared in over 40 books, solving crimes using logic and rationale. Her other detective, Miss Jane Marple, a typical British spinster, used her feminine powers of perception and insight to solve crimes. Miss Marple's character was evidently based on Christie's grandmother.

Christie wrote 66 mystery novels in 56 years. Some of her best-known works are *Murder on the Orient Express, Death on the Nile, 4:50 from Paddington* and *And Then There Were None.* Apart from detective novels, Christie also wrote her autobiography, in 1977, and several plays, of which *The Mousetrap* is the most famous, being the longest running play ever in London. It opened on 25 November 1952 and has run continuously since then at London's Ambassador Theatre. She also wrote romance novels under the pseudonym Mary Westmacott.

Christie always referred to herself as the "slow one" in the family and disliked editing or correcting her work. She developed her own style of writing by twisting the set standard of mystery novel writing and including the reader in solving the puzzle. Her method of revealing the murderer was always unique; sometime it might be the narrator, other times a group of people or a serial killer. She portrayed the world as a safe and conservative place. Society or deterioration of middle class values was never blamed for the murder; instead she provided a logical explanation of the events.

She became the president of the British Detection Club in 1967 and was made a Dame of the British Empire in 1971. Dame Agatha died of natural causes on January 12, 1976 in Wallingford, Oxfordshire, at the age of 85.

Samuel Clemens

GIVEN NAME: Samuel Langhorne Clemens
BORN: November 30, 1835
DIED: April 21, 1910
DROPPED OUT: Middle School

SAMUEL LANGHORNE CLEMENS is best known by his pen name, Mark Twain. He created a unique style of American writing using local themes and language. He was born in Florida, Missouri, to John and Jane Clemens. The family moved to Hannibal, Missouri, when Samuel was four. He entered public school there in 1840 but left when his father died in 1847. He went to work as an apprentice writer at the local newspaper to help pay off debts.

Clemens was enchanted by the Mississippi. He worked as a pilot on a steamboat and would have continued in that career had commercial traffic on the river not been stopped in 1861 because of the Civil War. His experiences during this time would later on be used in *Life on the Mississippi,* which he wrote in 1883. In 1861, Clemens traveled with his brother Orion, who had been appointed as secretary to the territorial governor, to Virginia City, Nevada. It was here that he took on the name, Mark Twain when he joined as a reporter of the *Territorial Enterprise.* His name, meaning two fathoms deep, safe water, in other words, referred to a safe place for a steamboat to drop anchor. His time in Virginia City formed the framework of his novel Roughing It. In 1886, he was commissioned by the *Sacramento Union* newspaper to write a series of letters describing his journey to Hawaii. The success of the letters led to a lecture series, which was again a huge success.

Clemens traveled to Europe and the Middle East and sent letters to be published in the Alta, California, newspaper; The letters became the foundation for his first book, *Innocents Abroad.* In 1870, Clemens married Olivia Langdon, moving first to Buffalo, New

York, and later to Hartford, Connecticut, where he lived most of his life.

Clemens, as Mark Twain, was famous for his wit and use of local vernacular in his novels. Some of his best-loved books are *Innocents Abroad, The Adventures of Tom Sawyer, The Adventures of Huckleberry Finn, Life on the Mississippi* and *A Connecticut Yankee in King Arthur's Court.* He wrote with rich humor and was adept at understanding local culture. He created a distinctive style of American literature. Mark Twain's defining novel, *The Adventures of Huckleberry Finn,* is considered one of the finest works of modern American literature.

Clemens was captivated by science and logic. He wrote *A Connecticut Yankee in King Arthur's Court,* about futuristic time travel, after spending time in Nikola Tesla's laboratory. In 1880, he anonymously published *1601: Conversation, as it was by the Social Fireside, in the Time of the Tudors* and acknowledged only in 1906 that he was its author. Another article, *The War Prayer,* was so controversial that it was not published until 1923. *Harper's Bazaar* rejected it in 1905 leading Clemens to comment, "I don't think the prayer will be published in my time. None but the dead are permitted to tell the truth."

In 1893, Clemens met Henry H Rogers, of Standard Oil, who helped him sort out his financial troubles. The two became close friends and Rogers's death in 1909 caused Clemens immense grief, as he was not in the best of health himself. He died less than a year later, outliving his wife and three of his four children. Ernest Hemmingway said of his work: "All modern American literature comes from one book by Mark Twain called *Huckleberry Finn*...all American writing comes from that. There was nothing before. There has been nothing as good since."

Jackie Collins

BIRTH NAME Jacqueline Jill Collins

BORN October 4, 1941

DROPPED OUT High School

JACKIE COLLINS, QUEEN of spirited, sexy novels based on celebrity lives, was born in London in 1941. She has one older sister, Joan, the Hollywood actress of Dynasty fame, and one younger brother, William. Her father, Joe Collins, was a theatrical agent and wanted both his daughters to join the theatre. Jackie's mother Elsa was a former dancer. Jackie started writing stories when she was eight years old, for her classmates, who were thrilled to read the steamy stories. Jackie was a playful girl, interested in entertaining others as well as having a good time herself.

Jackie Collins dropped out of school in her teens and her parents sent her to live in Los Angeles with Joan. On returning to England, Jackie married Wallace Austin in 1959. They were not happy together and, after the birth of their child Tracy, Wallace left Jackie and died soon after. Collins's second marriage was to Oscar Lerman, a nightclub and art gallery owner, with whom she had two daughters, Tiffany and Rory. The couple moved to Los Angeles so Collins could write books, surrounded by the world of movies and business, from which she took inspiration for her stories.

In 1968 Collins's first book, *The World is Full of Married Men*, equally shocked and delighted fans with her honest look at sexuality. The book was banned in Australia, giving Collins lots of media attention and making her successful overnight. She followed it up with more sensationalism, in *Stud*, in 1969, and the sequel *Bitch*, in 1979, focusing on the debauchery that came along with the glamour and high life of the movies. Her other books include *Sinners, The Love Killers, The World is Full of Divorced Women, Lovers and Gamblers, Chances* and the hugely successful *Hollywood Wives*, which was made into a miniseries starring Anthony Hopkins and Candice Bergen.

Lucky and *Chances* were turned into a six-hour miniseries staring Nicolette Sheridan and Sandra Bullock. *Lady Boss* was made into a miniseries in 1992, and starred Kim Delaney. Collins also wrote the screenplay for *Yesterday's Hero.*

The sequel to *Chances, Lucky* also rose to number one on the *New York Times* bestseller list. *Hollywood Husbands* was about the lives of the men of Hollywood and kept everyone guessing the characters' true identities. In *Rock Star,* Collins told the story of three super-stars of a rock band. In *Hollywood Kids,* she wrote about the power struggles, ambition, sex and drugs in which the younger generation of Hollywood celebrities was entangled. Her next book, *Vendetta,* published in 1996, again became a *New York Times* bestseller. *L.A. Connections, Dangerous Kiss, Lethal Seduction, Hollywood Wives: The New Generation* and *Deadly Seduction* also sold very well.

In 1998, Collins started her own show on television, *Jackie Collins Hollywood,* where she talked to a wide variety of stars.

Sometimes derided for being the queen of trash literature, Collins is an extremely successful novelist and has sold over 400 million copies of her books in over 40 countries.

Collins lives in Los Angeles and enjoys traveling to exotic places so she can include them in her books. She is also fond of photography and listening to soul music. Her husband died in the early 1990s after a long battle with cancer. Collins was devastated, but she continued with her work and spent time with her grandchildren. She has faced several personal losses through cancer and each time she has come out of it stronger. Jackie Collins is truly a survivor.

David Copperfield

BIRTH NAME David Seth Kotkin

BORN September 16, 1956

DROPPED OUT Fordham University

BORN IN METUCHEN, New Jersey, David Copperfield was passionate about magic from childhood. Learning card tricks from
his grandfather, he started performing when he was 12. He became
the youngest person ever admitted to the Society of American
Magicians. At 16, he was teaching a course in magic at New York
University.

Copperfield dropped out from Fordham University in New York
to play the lead in an original musical, *The Magic Man*. His performance brought him instant fame and it went on to become the
longest running musical ever staged in Chicago. ABC television,
recognizing his talent, made him the host of the show *The Magic
of ABC*. CBS then signed him for a series called *The Magic of David
Copperfield*, where his mind-boggling illusions before a live audience
catapulted him to fame. The show won several awards and David
Copperfield became a household name.

Copperfield mesmerizes viewers with his vanishing acts. In 1983,
he made the Statue of Liberty disappear. He walked through the
Great Wall of China and escaped from Alcatraz. He is the first il-
lusionist to fly without the use of wires. He once made 13 randomly
selected people from the audience of a live show disappear.

Copperfield's illusions are enormously popular with audiences.
As a result, he has become one of the highest paid entertainers in the
world. Yet he considers his greatest achievement to be Project Magic,
a rehabilitation program he developed to improve dexterity and motor skills in disabled patients using simple, sleight-of-hand magic.
The project is in operation in over 1,000 hospitals and 30 countries
across the world and has helped in motivating patients and building
their self-esteem.

Copperfield's Broadway show *Dreams and Nightmares* broke box-office records. His shows in Europe, North and South America and Asia have been staged in front of packed audiences. He has also been featured in magazines such as *Vanity Fair, Esquire, Architectural Digest* and *Paris Match*. The Library of Congress has named him a living legend. The French government has conferred on him the title Chevalier of Arts and Letters. He also appears on the stamps of four countries. Madame Tussaud's, in London, has honored Copperfield by making a replica of him in wax. He is also the only living magician to receive a star on the Hollywood Walk of Fame.

The International Museum and Library of the Conjuring Arts in Nevada houses Copperfield's vast collection of props, books, documents and related products to the art of magic and its history.

David Copperfield, one of the greatest illusionists of all time, has changed the way the world looks at magic and transformed it into a new art form with his modern approach. He has reinvented the art of magic and taken it to new heights with his innovative and imaginative style. Blending mystery and romance to create spectacular illusions, he has become a legendary figure in the world of entertainment.

$ **Millionaire Dropouts Trivia** $

Some of the highest-paid actors in the world (Tom Cruise, Tom Hanks, Jim Carrey, Johnny Depp and Leonardo Di Caprio) are all dropouts.

Simon Cowell

BIRTH NAME Simon Phillip Cowell

BORN October 7, 1959

DROPPED OUT High School

Simon Cowell is a music producer who rose to fame as a judge on the popular television programs *Pop Idol* and *American Idol*. His honest and often blunt assessment of contestants on the show made him a controversial but hugely successful judge.

Born in Brighton, England, the first time Cowell made a critical remark, according to his book *I Don't Mean to be Rude, But ...*, was at the tender age of four, when he looked at his mother's white fuzzy pillbox hat and said, "Mum, you look like a poodle." He dropped out of school when he was 16 and took a job in the mailroom at EMI Music Publishing, where his father, Eric Cowell, worked. The younger Cowell worked hard, eventually becoming a music producer, as he had an ear for music. He had a knack for identifying potential hits. BMG Records recognized his aptitude and took him on as an artists and repertoire (A&R) consultant in 1989.

Cowell became the man behind several pop success stories. He pioneered the emergence of famous bands like *Five* and *Westlife* and TV hits like cartoon puppets *Zig & Zag* and *The Teletubbies*. He claims that his biggest success was promoting the well-known pop-duo Robson and Jerome who hold the record for three consecutive number one singles on debut. By keenly following current trends and identifying talent, Cowell can today boast of sales of over 25 million albums, over 70 top-30 records and 17 number 1 singles.

When the TV series *Popstars* became a success, Cowell, along with Simon Fuller, decided to produce a musical talent show where the public would decide who should win. Auditions for the show numbered 10,000, becoming the most extensive auditions ever staged. The interactive nature of *Pop Idol* made it a popular show; the public watched and voted every Saturday evening. The final winner, Will

Young, got 4.6 million votes. The runner-up, Gareth Gates, got 4.1 million votes. Will Young's debut album *Evergreen/Anything is Possible* broke records as well as registering sales worth over $2 million. Gareth Gates' album, with sales of 1 million records, became a fast selling debut album.

Cowell became a celebrity, too, and the *Sunday Times* Rich List estimated that he earned $33.5 million in just a year, following the success of the *Pop Idol*. *American Idol*, the U.S. version of the show, was also an incredible success. The show's host was Ryan Seacrest. Performers Kelly Clarkson, Clay Aiken and Ruben Studdard became stars overnight. The panel of judges, which included Cowell, Paula Abdul and Randy Jackson, came to be loved or hated by the audiences; by the end of the first season, Cowell got a contract that made him the highest paid judge on the panel.

The ability to recognize and promote potential talent has made Simon Cowell a successful producer, judge and promoter of TV shows and music albums. He has proved that everybody stands to gain when there's rich artistic talent waiting to be tapped.

$ **Millionaire Dropouts Trivia** $

Some of the highest-paid actresses in the world (Cameron Diaz, Nicole Kidman, Angelina Jolie and Drew Barrymore) are all dropouts.

Cindy Crawford

BIRTH NAME Cynthia Ann Crawford
BORN February 20, 1966
DROPPED OUT Northwestern University

CINDY CRAWFORD IS a highly successful model and actress. She is also an astute businesswoman and celebrity spokesperson who endorses several products.

Born in DeKalb, Illinois, Crawford had a tough childhood. Her brother Jeff died of leukemia when Cindy was just ten years old. Her parents divorced when she was still a teenager. She was a good student at school and was her high school valedictorian. On being awarded a scholarship, she entered Northwestern University to study chemical engineering but dropped out after the first semester to pursue a career in modeling.

Blessed with authentic good looks and a perfect physique, Crawford quickly became a successful model. She appeared in a number of commercials and on the magazine covers of *Vogue, W, Elle* and *Allure*. She was seen alongside famous models like Naomi Campbell and Claudia Schiffer. In 1997, a *Shape* magazine survey named her as the second most beautiful woman in the world (after Demi Moore). *People Magazine* named her one of the 50 most beautiful people. *Playboy* named her as one of the ten sexiest stars of the century in 1998.

Crawford, a shrewd businesswoman, signed multiyear contracts with several well known companies and became the most photographed and recognized face in the world. She produced a workout video called *Cindy Crawford—Shape Your Body* that made it to the top of the health and fitness charts and sold over two million copies in the U.S. alone. She published her book, *Cindy Crawford's Basic Face: A Makeup Workbook,* and started her own company, Crawdaddy Inc. She has marketed her own perfumes—Cindy Crawford Joyful,

Cindy Crawford Waterfalls and Cindy Crawford Feminine. After establishing herself as a supermodel, Crawford hosted *MTV Style,* Fox TV's *Concert for Life* and ABC's popular show *Sex with Cindy Crawford.*

In 1995, she was named the highest paid actress by *Forbes Magazine.* That same year she costarred with William Baldwin in the film *Fair Game.* Although the film was not a big hit, she continued with her acting career and performed small roles in *The Secret of My Success* and *Sesame Street: Elmopalooza.* She has had roles in *Unzipped, Catwalk* and *Beautopia.*

A mother of two children, Crawford started her own online store, babystyle.com, in 1999. Putting her talent to best use, she has proved to be successful not only as a supermodel, but also as a businesswoman with great foresight and marketing skills, proving that she is a perfect blend of beauty and brains.

Dale Earnhardt

BIRTH NAME Ralph Dale Earnhardt
BORN April 29, 1951
DIED February 18, 2001
DROPPED OUT High School

DALE EARNHARDT WAS born in Kannapolis, North Carolina, into a racing family. His father, Ralph, was a successful driver who died of a heart attack in 1973 while working on his race car. Dale dropped out of high school in the ninth grade to focus on a career in cars and racing. As a teenager, to earn money he started racing hobby-class cars at night and worked making improvements on them during the day.

In 1975, Earnhardt began his career in stock car racing, driving for Ed Negre and later for Rod Osterlund. When the latter's regular driver, Dave Marcis, left to start his own team in 1979, Osterlund selected Earnhardt to race in the Winston Cup. He won the Rookie of the Year Award at the competition. It was the turning point of his career.

In 1981, Rod Osterlund sold his team to Richard Childress. Earnhardt and Childress formed a good partnership. They were determined to win the Winston Cup Championship conducted by the National Association of Stock Car Automobile Racing (NASCAR). Their first success was in 1986 and from then on; the triumphs came one after another, with Earnhardt accumulating six titles over nine seasons. He won the prestigious Daytona 500 on his twentieth attempt in 1998. He was also included in the list of 50 greatest drivers in NASCAR history, along with his father.

Earnhardt's aggressive driving style earned him the nickname The Intimidator. His style on the racetrack was just part of his winning strategy, not an indication of who he was as a person. To Earnhardt, success was everything. He said "second place is the first loser."

Earnhardt was an innovative driver. In addition to being excellent at drafting, which exploits the fact two cars that are lined up and closely spaced go faster than a single car, he created a variation called side-drafting.

Winning seven NASCAR championships in his career, Earnhardt had total prize winnings exceeding $41 million. An estimated 40–50 percent of the memorabilia sold at NASCAR races was Earnhardt's. He drove the number 3 car for almost his entire career, sponsored first by Wrangler Jeans and later by GM Goodwrench.

Off the track, Earnhardt was a private person who enjoyed working on his Kannapolis farm. He was generous by nature and was involved in charitable work. He was married three times and had four children. His sons Kerry and Dale Jr. follow the family tradition of racing.

Dale Earnhardt died in a crash on the final lap of the 2001 Daytona 500, shocking fans across the country. Earnhardt was one of the most dashing sportsmen on the car racing tracks in the U.S. He played an important role in making stock car racing a national obsession in the country. His life is a blazing story of commitment and passion for a sport that revolves around speed.

$ **Millionaire Dropouts Trivia** $

America's first billionaire, John D Rockefeller Sr., was a high school dropout.

Albert Einstein

BIRTH NAME Albert Einstein
BORN March 14, 1879
DIED April 18, 1955
DROPPED OUT Luitpold Gymnasium

ALBERT EINSTEIN WAS born in Ulm, Germany, and grew up in Munich, studying at the Luitpold Gymnasium. In 1894, his family moved to Pavia, Italy, while Albert remained in Munich to attend school. He dropped out after a term to join his family and eventually earned his secondary school diploma from Aarau, Switzerland in 1896.

On earning a teaching diploma from the Swiss Federal Institute of Technology (Eidgenössische Technische Hochschule) in Zurich, Einstein became a Swiss citizen. Unable to find a teaching position, he instead joined the Swiss Patent Office in 1902. While working there, Einstein earned his doctorate in 1905, the year now known as Annus Mirablis (Latin for year of wonders) because of the publication of four papers that revolutionized modern physics, all authored by Einstein. These papers, on Brownian motion, the photoelectric effect and special relativity, provided a theoretical basis to explain experimental results that had long baffled physicists. In one of the two special relativity papers he applied the equation $E = mc^2$ to the energy binding of the atomic nucleus for the first time.

Einstein preseted the theory of general relativity in a series of lectures in 1915, replacing Newton's law of gravity with the Field Equation, which envisions gravity not as a force but rather as a consequence of the curvature of space–time. Einstein lived to see some experimental support for general relativity, but it was still controversial at his death. Today it is established fact, with its minute effects a necessary part of the calculations that allow the GPS system to remain accurate over time.

From 1911 to 1914, Einstein was a professor at the University of Zurich, later at the University of Prague and then at ETH Zurich. He moved to Berlin in 1914 and after becoming a German citizen joined the Prussian Academy of Sciences. In 1921, he won the Nobel Prize for his paper on the photoelectric effect. He was the director of the Kaiser Wilhelm Institute for Physics until 1933.

Einstein's work was often discredited in Germany because of rising anti-Semitism; when Hitler came to power in 1933 Einstein renounced his German citizenship. He moved to Princeton, New Jersey, where he joined the Institute for Advanced Study and concentrated on the unification of the laws of physics. He became a U.S. citizen in 1940.

In his private life Einstein was a modest man who liked to sail and play the violin. He regarded himself a pacifist, except for the brief time during World War II when he instigated the Manhattan Project by writing to President Roosevelt urging the development of nuclear fission to counteract Hitler's plan of building the first atomic bomb. After the war, Einstein promoted the cause of international disarmament and was part of the World Government Movement. He was also a humanitarian and felt that Gandhi's views were the most enlightened of all the political men of his time.

Albert Einstein has become a pop culture icon in contemporary times and his name is a synonym for intelligence. He explored new frontiers of science with his endless curiosity and thirst for knowledge but always considered imagination to be more important than knowledge. Einstein is often acknowledged as the greatest scientist of the twentieth century. He propounded the theory of relativity and made important contributions to the growth of quantum mechanics, string theory and cosmology.

William Faulkner

BIRTH NAME William Falkner
BORN September 25, 1897
DIED July 6, 1962
DROPPED OUT High School

WILLIAM FAULKNER, NOBEL Prize–winning American author, was born William Falkner (without the *u*) in 1897 to Murry and Maud Butler Falkner in New Albany, Mississippi, the first of four sons. His great-grandfather Col. William Clark Falkner served in the Confederate Army, founded a railway and wrote a popular romantic novel.

Faulkner, the spelling he chose as an adult, set his novels in his native South. However, he joined the RAF in Canada, seeking military glory in World War I.

Although the war ended before he finished his training, Faulkner alluded to his being a war veteran. His time spent in training was fodder for his first novel, *Soldier's Pay*, written in 1925. Some of his most famous novels are *The Sound and the Fury, As I Lay Dying, Light in August, The Unvanquished, The Wild Palms, Absalom, Absalom!* and *Go Down, Moses*. Besides novels, Faulkner also wrote many short stories.

Faulkner entered the University of Mississippi, in Oxford, in 1919, even though he had not completed high school. As a student, Faulkner was involved in writing poems and short stories for the campus newspaper; he also founded *The Marionettes*, a dramatic club in the university. Faulkner dropped out of school again, in November 1920, after three semesters.

Faulkner's best known novel, *The Sound and the Fury*, was published in 1929. It was the story of an aristocratic southern family and its decline, narrated by four brothers.

Faulkner married his childhood friend Estelle Oldham in April 1929 after she divorced her first husband, Cornell Franklin. With her two children, Malcolm and Victoria, they lived in Oxford. Faulkner, trying to increase his earnings while working nights at a power plant, wrote his masterpiece, *As I Lay Dying* in six weeks. He focused again on a family and the destiny of its members, but this time the characters were poor farm laborers.

In April 1930, *The Forum* published the short story "A Rose for Emily." That was followed by the publication of other stories in major magazines including *Collier's* and the *Saturday Evening Post*. Also in 1930, *Sanctuary*, which had earlier been rejected by publishers, was accepted and went on to become his best-selling novel at the time.

William and Estelle's first child, Alabama, born in 1931, survived only a few days. Deeply influenced by the loss, Faulkner wrote a collection of short stories *These 13*, and began on *Light in August*, a novel about race and how it affects relationships. In 1933 William and Estelle had a baby girl, Jill.

In 1936, Faulkner wrote *Absalom, Absolom!* He was elected to the National Institute of Arts and Letters in 1939. He was awarded the Nobel Prize for Literature for 1949 and Pulitzer Prizes for *A Fable* in 1955 and posthumously for *The Reivers*.

Faulkner was a writer-in-residence at the University of Virginia for several years. After a fall from his horse, Faulkner was taken to the hospital. He died of a heart attack in 1962 and was buried in St. Peter's Cemetery in Oxford.

Tom Ford

BIRTH NAME Tom Ford

BORN August 27, 1961

DROPPED OUT High School

TOM FORD WAS born in Austin, Texas and grew up in Santa Fe, New Mexico. Interested in all aspects of design from an early age, Ford moved to New York when he was a teenager and enrolled in a course in art history at New York University. He switched to study interior design at the Parsons School of Design in New York, studied there and at Parsons in Paris, finishing up in New York.

In 1986, he started working for designer Cathy Hardwick in New York and within two years became the Design Director at Perry Ellis. In 1990, Dawn Mello, Gucci's creative director, selected him to design ready-to-wear for its women's division, in Milan, and two years later Ford became design director at Gucci. He has been credited with turning around Gucci from a staid and stuck-in-the-rut brand to a fashion powerhouse by the late 1990s.

Taking a hands-on approach at Gucci, Ford created a particular style of clothing for the fashion house and worked to improve its brand. He upgraded the look and image of the company's store design and advertisements. Some of his advertisements received a lot of attention for their controversial content and depiction. Ford's marketing style started a craze for owning Gucci bags and other accessories covered with the Gucci logo, a type of presentation that has been copied by many other designers.

Under Ford's leadership, Gucci went on to acquire the Yves Saint Laurent label in 2000. Ford became the creative director for YSL, too. After ten productive years at Gucci, Ford decided to leave in 2004 to pursue his goal of directing films. He then announced that he would be designing his own fashion line.

Celebrities love Ford's sexy, sophisticated line of designer wear and they flaunt the Gucci label at many prestigious award functions.

Each season the world waited with bated breath to see the new collection. The Council of Fashion Designers of America named Ford its designer of the year in 1995. His clients include Madonna, Bianca Jagger, Gwyneth Paltrow, Jennifer Lopez and Trudie Styler.

In May 2004, Ford joined Sothebys in Paris as an advisor. Meanwhile he is taking on acting and directing jobs in Hollywood.

Tom Ford is one of the most influential designers in the world of haute couture. He saved Gucci from the brink of bankruptcy and made it a thriving, vibrant brand by creating an elegant and sexy style that has become the favorite of celebrities. His emphasis on exploiting the power of a brand name to enhance image and sales has ushered in a new era for designers in the fashion world.

$ **Millionaire Dropouts Trivia** $

The U.S. penny and quarter-dollar coins, as well as the one, five, twenty, one hundred and thousand-dollar bills all include images of dropouts.

Laird Hamilton

BIRTH NAME Laird John Zerfas
BORN March 2, 1964
DROPPED OUT High School

LAIRD HAMILTON WAS born in San Francisco but grew up in Oahu, Hawaii, where he learned to surf. His adoptive father is the legendary Bill Hamilton, a big wave surfer of the 1960s. JoAnn Zyriek, Laird's mother, is also a surfer. Laird experienced racism in school, being the only blond-haired boy; for him the ocean became the place to even scores. Eventually he dropped out of school and moved to California, where he was better able to fit in. He even used his looks to his advantage by becoming a model.

Returning to Hawaii in the late 1980s, Hamilton made a statement with his innovative, powerful and aggressive style of surfing. To surf waves that were too big to catch by paddling he used jet skis and conquered a challenging spot on Maui called Peahi, now renamed Jaws. This area has become a favorite haunt for surfers keen to try out new big-wave surfing techniques.

Hamilton has been responsible for introducing several new styles of surfing. Using his tow-in surfing technique, which many of his peers considered cheating, he conquered the Teahupoo surf spot in Tahiti on August 17, 2000. This one act made him a legend in surfing circles and put him on the cover of *Surfer Magazine*. The foil board technique, which combines hydrofoil technology with surfboards, is another innovation of his. Besides surfing, he excels in other water sports, including windsurfing, water skiing and jet skiing. Hamilton has played an important role in improving windsurfing techniques and increasing the popularity of the sport. He windsurfed between the Hawaiian islands of Oahu and Kauai in 2003, setting a speed record.

Hamilton's physical build has contributed in a big way to his success. At six-three, he can control the larger waves more easily than smaller surfers can . He has been featured in several magazines and was named one of the 50 most beautiful people by *People Magazine* in 1996.

Fame has taken Hamilton beyond the world of professional surfing. He has performed stunts for movies, including *Waterworld, Die Another Day, Night Waves, Totally Committed* and *Five Summer Stories.* He starred in North Shore, a movie about an unethical surfer. Besides acting and performing stunts, Hamilton provides expert advice to film and television companies on the technicalities of shooting in surf.

Hamilton excelled through his persistent experimentation with new methods of surfing. He has never been interested in entering competitions and views surfing as he does life, a challenge to master and then move on to new and bigger quests.

Laird Hamilton is today the most celebrated big wave surfer in the world. He is famous for his innovative methods and use of modern technology to push the limits of physical endurance and achieve breathtaking results.

$ **Millionaire Dropouts Trivia** $

America's first millionaire, John Jacob Astor, was a high school dropout.

William Hanna

BIRTH NAME William Denby Hanna
BORN July 14, 1910
DIED March 22, 2001
DROPPED OUT Compton Junior College

WILLIAM HANNA, CREATIVE force behind famous cartoons like Yogi Bear and Scooby Doo, was born in Melrose, New Mexico. His father was a construction supervisor for the Santa Fe Railway; so the family moved quite often. They finally settled in Los Angeles in 1919. William was a talented artist. He inherited his creative skills from the maternal side of the family, which included a number of writers who influenced William in his creative choices both in school and later. William joined The Boy Scouts in Los Angeles and was actively involved in the organization for the remainder of his life.

Hanna decided to become a structural engineer. He enrolled in Compton Junior College, majoring in engineering and journalism, but dropped out because of the Great Depression, working to help his father in the construction of the Pantages Theatre. In 1931, he joined the Harman-Ising cartoon studio, providing story and layout ideas to *Loony Tunes* and *Merrie Melodies*. In 1937, MGM decided to stop outsourcing its cartoon production and formed its own animation unit. Hanna shifted to MGM, becoming director for the *Captain and the Kids* series.

It was here that Hanna met Joseph Barbera and formed a long and successful partnership with him. They were most popular for their *Tom and Jerry* series, which won seven Academy Awards. Hanna and Barbera formed their own company, Hanna–Barbera Productions, in 1957, when MGM closed its animation production unit. They decided to focus on producing cartoons specifically for television, making some of the best-loved cartoon shows and creating characters like Huckleberry Hound, Yogi Bear, the Flintstones, Johnny Quest, the Banana Splits and Scooby Doo.

The Flintstones was the first half-hour animated sitcom on television and went on to become one of the world's most watched shows for the six years it aired. Hanna–Barbera Productions was the most successful television animation studio by the late 1960s.

The company also made animated films, including *A Man Called Flintstone,* in 1966, *Charlotte's Web,* in 1972 and *Heidi's Song,* in 1982. Hanna was an executive producer on *The Flintstones in Viva Rock Vegas,* in 2000, and for *Scooby Doo,* which was completed after his death.

Often referred to disparagingly as the poor man's Disney, the Hanna–Barbera collaboration led to the making of the some of the most memorable cartoon characters. Together they produced over 3000 cartoons. Hanna stayed actively involved with cartoons, even after selling Hanna–Barbera Productions to Taft Communications, co-producing *Once Upon a Forest.* One of the last hits of the company was *Dexter's Laboratory.*

William Hanna and Joseph Barbera received their star on the Hollywood Walk of Fame in 1976 and were inducted into the Television Academy Hall of Fame in 1983. Hanna married Violet Blanch Wogatzke in 1936; they had two children, a son, David, and a daughter, Bonnie. Hanna died in 2001 in Los Angeles. William Hanna was a successful man of his own making, relying on strong natural talents and turning whatever came his way into opportunities.

Harry Houdini

BIRTH NAME Erik Weisz
BORN March 24, 1874
DIED October 31, 1926
DROPPED OUT Elementary School

HARRY HOUDINI WAS born as Erik Weisz in Budapest, Hungary. His father, Mayer Samuel Weisz, was a religious scholar and teacher. When he was young, the family went through hard times financially. His father moved first to Appleton, Wisconsin, where he served as a rabbi for a few years. Young Harry Weiss (the Americanized form of his Hungarian nickname Ehrie, and the spelling given the family's last name by an immigration clerk) left home at 12, hopping a freight train for Kansas City, hoping to earn money to help support the family. He worked at odd jobs and made his way east to New York City. In 1887, he rejoined his family, who had moved to New York by then.

Harry started studying magic and took part in various athletic events, too. His idol was the father of the modern magic act, the French magician Robert Houdin, who had written *The Memoirs of Robert Houdin, Ambassador, Author, and Conjuror, Written by Himself*. Harry called himself Houdini when he started performing in public at 17.

Houdini's father died in 1892; Houdini was 18. He performed, first with his brother, at amusement parks and dime museums, replacing his brother in the act when he married Beatrice (Bess) Raymond, a singer. Initially specializing in card tricks, by 1895 they started introducing larger illusions, such as switching places in a trunk.

In 1899, Houdini met Martin Beck, a showman who encouraged him to focus on his escape act. Beck booked him on the Orpheum vaudeville circuit, leading to a tour of Europe. He returned to the U.S. famous for his escape tricks, freeing himself from handcuffs, chains and ropes. He staged public stunts everywhere he went, escaping from handcuffs provided by local police, jumping, manacled, off bridges, escaping from a milk can full of water. His most famous act, was the "Chinese water torture cell," in which he would dangle upside down in a locked glass cabinet full of water. He put in hours to perfect his stunts, holding his breath in a specially built tub to practice for his underwater acts.

After World War I, Houdini began a film career, acting first in a movie serial before starting his own film company in 1921. He acted in five more silent films, none of them commercial successes.

After the death of Houdini's mother in 1920, he started exposing people who claimed to be psychics and mediums, using his knowledge of stage magic to expose their tricks. He joined a committee of American scientists to protect people from being duped by such healers.

Houdini died tragically at 52. On a visit to McGill University, to give a lecture on spiritualism, he was asked if he could withstand a blow to the stomach. Before he could prepare by tightening his stomach muscles, a student hit him. He recovered from the blow but died of peritonitis from a ruptured appendix.

Houdini had made a pact with his wife Bess that he would contact her after death if possible and deliver a prearranged message. Bess held a séance for ten years every Halloween; but in 1936 she put out a candle beside Houdini's photograph, saying, "ten years is long enough to wait for any man."

Peter Jennings

BIRTH NAME Peter Charles Archibald
Ewart Jennings

BORN July 29, 1938

DIED August 7, 2005

DROPPED OUT High School

PETER JENNINGS WAS born in Toronto, Ontario, Canada. His father, Charles Jennings, was head of the news department at the Canadian Broadcasting Corporation. When he was 9, Peter anchored a kids' show, *Peter's People,* for CBC Radio. He dropped out of high school and worked as a bank-teller and a disc jockey. Canada's first private TV network, CTV, noticed his coverage of a local train wreck and asked him to co-anchor its late-night *CTV National News.* He worked for CTV through 1964, covering the civil rights movement, the assassination of John F. Kennedy and other important events of the era. He joined ABC in 1965, anchoring *Peter Jennings with the News.* At 26, he was the youngest American network news anchor to date, but that worked against him, competing as he was against the mature and respected Walter Cronkite, Chet Huntley and David Brinkley. He lost the anchor slot in 1968.

Determined to make a comeback, Jennings stayed on at ABC as a foreign correspondent, covering the Middle East and the Lebanese civil war. After the Shah of Iran fled the country, Jennings was the first to get an interview with Iran's Ayatollah Khomeini. He also covered the massacre of Israeli athletes by Palestinian terrorists at the Munich Olympics. In 1978, he started anchoring *ABC World News Tonight* along with Frank Reynolds from Washington and Max Robinson from Chicago. From 1983 through April 2005, he was the sole anchor, covering major news events live as they unfolded. He spent more than 60 hours on the air following the attack on the World Trade Center on September 11, 2001. The coverage earned ABC News the Peabody and Dupont awards.

Jennings was "in Berlin in the 1960s when the Berlin Wall was going up, and there again, in the late 1980s when it came down," according to his official ABC biography. Reporting from over 50 locations around the globe, he played a major role in covering the conflict in Bosnia, the war in Iraq, India–Pakistan relations, the crisis in Haiti and the drug trade in Central and South America. His *Peter Jennings Reporting* earned him several awards, including the 2004 Edward R. Murrow award for best documentary for *The Kennedy Assassination—Beyond Conspiracy.*

Over 175 million Americans watched *ABC 2000*, his coverage of Millennium Eve on December 31, 1999. It was the biggest live telecast ever. During his tenure as an anchor and senior editor of *World News Tonight,* his experience in the Middle East proved to be invaluable. ABC's coverage of the 1991 Gulf War and the 2003 War in Iraq greatly benefited by his experience and understanding of affairs in these countries. He also tackled several domestic issues like education, health care and tobacco. He received several major awards in his career, including 16 Emmys, two George Foster Peabody Awards and several Alfred I. Dupont–Columbia University Awards.

Jennings died in 2005 after battling lung cancer. ABC mourned his death with several special shows.

Peter Jennings ushered in a new era in television journalism, with his in-depth coverage of challenging and controversial issues.

Herman Melville

BIRTH NAME Herman Melville

BORN August 1, 1819

DIED September 28, 1891

DROPPED OUT Albany School

HEERMAN MELVILLE, FAMED American writer of *Moby-Dick*, was born in 1819 in New York City to Allan and Maria Ganesvoort Melville. The Melvilles were a family of patriots, with both grandfathers in the Army. The family moved to Albany, where Herman enrolled in the Albany Academy but left after his father's death in 1832, to work as a bank clerk to help support his family. Herman had been a good but slow student and educated himself from then on. After a bout with scarlet fever, his eyesight was also permanently affected.

After a few years of drifting and looking for jobs, Melville decided to sail and see the world. He signed up in 1840 as a seaman on a whaling ship, the *Acushnet*, sailing to the Pacific. On returning in 1844, he was encouraged by his family to write of his adventures. In 1846, he wrote *Typee*, about the Typee tribe in Polynesia. The publishers considered it too good to be true and rejected it. It was published after some revision and authentication in 1846. Later that year, he followed with a sequel, *Omoo: A Narrative of Adventure in the South Seas*, about his time spent on the sea and on the island of Tahiti. He sailed on the *Charles and Henry*, a Nantucket whaler, which served as the setting of the third and weakest of his Polynesian books, *Mardi*.

In 1847, Melville married Elizabeth Shaw in Boston. Elizabeth was the daughter of the chief justice of Massachusetts, Lemuel Shaw, a close friend of Melville's father. Melville wrote his next two books, *Redburn* and *White-Jacket*, in quick succession in 1849 to increase his income after the failure of *Mardi*.

Moby-Dick was Melville's masterpiece. He achieved maximum personal satisfaction from writing the book, although it was not well received by critics. *Moby-Dick* became popular a generation after Melville's death. In 1852, he wrote *Pierre; or, the Ambiguities.* The book did not connect with readers, who thought the content was in bad taste. Melville published some short stories in 1856 under the title, *The Piazza Tales,* while also working on *The Confidence Man.* A century later this would be considered his second masterpiece; *The Confidence Man* was his most modern and American novel in its setting, characters, culture and stereotypes.

In late 1856, feeling ill and depressed, Melville decided to travel again. He visited Scotland, England, the Mediterranean, the Holy Land, Greece, Turkey, Egypt, Italy, Germany and Switzerland, returning after eight months. In an effort to boost his income, he gave lectures from 1857 to 1860, speaking about his travels to the South Pacific. He began working as a customs agent at the waterfront in New York City in 1866 to supplement his dwindling income from book sales and also relied on money from his wife's family.

In his later years, Melville became interested in poetry, avidly reading Shelley, Tennyson and other poets. In 1876, he published *Clarel A Poem and Pilgrimage in the Holy Land,* a contemplative poem based on his travels to the Holy Land. It did not receive favorable reviews, but it had a cathartic effect on Melville, who finally sorted out his finances so that he could buy books and privately publish small editions of his works. His next poetry book, *John Marr and Other Sailors,* was published in 1888.

Herman Melville died in New York City, after a prolonged illness, in 1891 and was interred in Woodlawn Cemetery in New York. The short novel *Billy Budd* was published after his death and also made into an opera. A quiet man, Melville relied on his works to speak for him, never letting go of opportunities to open his mind to new places, cultures and thoughts.

Rosa Parks

BIRTH NAME Rosa Louise McCauley
BORN February 4, 1913
DIED October 24, 2005
DROPPED OUT Alabama State Teacher's College

ROSA MCCAULEY WAS born in Tuskegee, Alabama, to James and Leona McCauley, and grew up in Pine Level, Alabama, on her grandparents' farm. She entered the Montgomery Industrial School for Girls when she was 11 and later switched to the Alabama State Teacher's College for tenth and eleventh grades, only to drop out to care for her sick grandmother. The Montgomery Industrial School was founded by forward-thinking, liberal women who believed in the philosophy of self-worth. The education that she received here along with her mother's influence helped Rosa grow up strong, independent and fearless.

Rosa married Raymond Parks and they set up home in Montgomery, becoming members of the National Association for the Advancement of Colored People (NAACP), to help improve the conditions of African-Americans. She was actively involved in organizing voter registration drives in the city as well as in other civic and religious events. In 1943, Mrs. Parks was elected secretary of the Montgomery chapter of the NAACP.

In 1955 Mrs. Parks was working at a department store. She received worldwide attention for her refusal to vacate her seat on a public bus for a white passenger. She was arrested, tried and convicted for violating the local ordinance. Her act of civil disobedience triggered a boycott of all city buses that lasted over a year. Dr. Martin Luther King Jr. set up the Montgomery Improvement Association and rose to prominence due to his involvement in the boycott. In 1956, the Supreme Court overturned the Montgomery ordinance defining racial segregation as unconstitutional and outlawed segregation on public transportation.

110   www.MillionaireDropouts.com

Mrs. Parks's act of disobedience stemmed from simply wanting to be treated with decency and dignity. It marked a turning point in the battle for racial equality by African-Americans and was the precursor to the emergence of Dr. Martin Luther King Jr. as a national leader of the civil rights movement.

Mrs. Parks lost her job as a result of her action and received constant death threats; the couple decided to move to Detroit in 1957. After struggling for eight years, Mrs. Parks got a job as an administrative assistant to U.S. Congressman John F. Conyers Jr., for whom she worked till 1987. She established the Rosa and Raymond Parks Institute for Self-Development to motivate the younger generation to achieve their goals.

During her lifetime, Mrs. Parks received several awards, including the Spingarn Medal in 1970, the Martin Luther King Jr. Award in 1980 and the Presidential Medal of Freedom in 1996. A road in Montgomery is named in her honor. Rosa Parks died on October 24, 2005 of natural causes in her Detroit home.

Mrs. Park's protest brought about dramatic changes in the rights of African-Americans in the South. A shy and quiet person, once she decided on something, she was determined to stand her ground and face the consequences with dignity and courage. A pioneer in the struggle for racial equality, Rosa Parks wished to be remembered as a person who "wanted to be free and wanted others to be free."

Sam Phillips

BIRTH NAME Samuel Cornelius Phillips
BORN January 5, 1923
DIED July 30, 2003
DROPPED OUT Coffee High School

SAM PHILLIPS WAS instrumental in the emergence of rock and roll music in the 1950s. He brought it to the mainstream and changed forever the world of music. Phillips launched several well-known artists, but the discovery that ensured his fame was Elvis Presley.

Phillips grew up in Florence, Alabama, on a cotton farm. Dropping out of Coffee High School to help support his mother and aunt in 1945, he moved to Memphis to work as a radio announcer and maintenance and broadcast engineer at WREC. Yearning to do more than just listen to music, he set up the Memphis Recording Service in January, 1950. In 1952 he formed Sun Records.

Phillips recorded rhythm and blues artists like James Cotton, Howlin' Wolf, Rosco Gordon, Little Milton and B. B. King from 1950 to 1954. The rhythm and blues genre consisted entirely of black musicians, but Phillips wanted to find a white singer who had a special sound. He found that singer in Elvis Presley, who came to the studio to record "My Happiness" and "That's When Your Heartaches Begin" as a gift for his mother's birthday. Recognizing instantly the emotional depth and variation in Presley's voice, Phillips decided to sign him and promote his career.

Presley's success opened the doors to thousands of hopeful singers. Some of Phillips's phenomenal success stories were Jerry Lee Lewis, Johnny Cash, Roy Orbison and Carl Perkins; but several others, such as Charlie Rich and Sonny Burgess were also successful. In 1955, because of severe financial strain, Phillips sold Elvis Presley's contract to RCA Records for $35,000.

Phillips was able to bring together different streams of music, including blues, rhythm and blues, country and gospel, and provide musicians with a complete package from production to marketing. His studio's distinctive sound quality and the relaxed atmosphere of the recording sessions were its keys to success. Phillips was responsible for bringing out *Rocket 88* by Jackie Brenston and Ike Turner's Delta Cats band in 1951, which is widely credited as being the first rock and roll record.

His contribution to the music industry has been so singular that during his lifetime Phillips was inducted into the Rock and Roll Hall of Fame, the Alabama Music Hall of Fame and the Blues Hall of Fame. In 1991, he received a Grammy Trustees Award.

Besides his involvement in Sun Records, Phillips made a fortune in the hotel business, after he invested in the local Holiday Hotel, which eventually grew into the Holiday Inn chain. Phillips died of respiratory failure at Francis Hospital in Memphis in July 2003, at 80. Sam Phillips was a humble man and remained modest about his role as a pioneer in the rock and roll industry.

$ **Millionaire Dropouts Trivia** $

**Elijah McCoy, who invented the ironing board as well as a lubrication system for steam engines, was a dropout. He attracted notice among his African-American contemporaries.
Booker T. Washington, in Story of the Negro (1909), recognized him as having produced more patents than any other African-American inventor up to that time.**

Will Rogers

BIRTH NAME William Penn Adair Rogers
BORN November 4, 1879
DIED August 15, 1935
DROPPED OUT High School

WILL ROGERS WAS born in the Cherokee Nation Indian Territory, near what is now Oologah, Oklahoma, and grew up on the family ranch. His parents were part Cherokee. He was one of eight children and learned to use the lasso to work with cattle on the ranch. He became so adept at using the lasso that he eventually made it to the *Guinness Book of World Records* for throwing three lassos at once.

Rogers dropped out of school in tenth grade to work as a cowboy. Five years later, he started performing rope-tricks in traveling shows, reaching South Africa, New Zealand and Australia. In 1904, he performed at the World Fairs in St Louis and New York City. After the fairs ended, he toured vaudeville circuits in America, Canada and Europe for the next decade. He started with rope tricks, but he added jokes and patter to the act. His keen observations about people, their lives and the countryside made him hugely popular as a performer. His style was simple and the audience loved his intelligent and witty remarks. He soon became more famous for his brand of humor than his rope feats.

Rogers acted in over 50 silent films and 21 talking pictures as well as Broadway productions. He was a top-box office star, voted the most popular male actor in Hollywood in 1934. He traveled the world, exchanging views with world leaders, people in the arts, and others. Although he had dropped out of school, he was always keen to learn and it was his thirst for knowledge that transformed him from a cowboy to a writer, humorist and a political commentator. He wrote six books and over 4,000 syndicated columns in addition to being a radio commentator. World leaders sought his opinion and he was a guest at the White House.

His life was cut short when he died in an air crash in 1935, at the age of 55, together with his aviator friend Wiley Post, near Point Barrow, Alaska.

It was Will Roger's quest for learning, combined with hard work that made him so successful and popular. Will Roger's wit, political writings and sayings are still relevant. His memory is kept alive by the musical *The Will Rogers Follies*, which introduces him to new audiences. The Will Rogers Institute offers funds for research in pulmonary diseases, and is a fitting memorial to the man who always thought of himself as a caring member of the human race, offering money to disaster victims and raising money for the Red Cross and Salvation Army.

$ **Millionaire Dropouts Trivia** $

**"I have watched all the dropouts
who made their own rules" is a line
in Ozzy Osbourne's song, "Crazy Train."
Ozzy is a high school dropout, as is his daughter.**

Valentina Tereshkova

BIRTH NAME Valentina Vladimirovna Tereshkova
BORN March 6, 1937
DROPPED OUT High School

VALENTINA TERESHKOVA BECAME a national heroine with her flight aboard the Vostok 6, becoming the first woman to fly in outer space. Born in Maslennikova, USSR, Valentina was not able to attend school until she was 10 because her family had financial problems. She left school at 16 to work in a textile factory as a loom operator. In her spare time, she studied cotton-spinning technology at the Light Industry Technical School.

A member of the local Aeroclub, Tereshkova was a skilled parachutist; it was her skill here that led her to space. The Soviet Union wanted to beat the U.S. in sending the first woman to space and began recruiting parachutists in 1961, as there were no women pilots at that time. Tereshkova was one of the five chosen for training as cosmonauts and the only one to travel to space.

Because of Cold War tensions with the U.S., the Soviet government conducted their cosmonaut training under utmost secrecy. Tereshkova did not even tell her mother the truth about her selection, telling her instead that she was training for a skydiving team. Her mother eventually learned of the truth only after the flight was announced on the radio. The government did not reveal the identities of the other women in the cosmonaut program until the 1980s.

The Soviet Air Force conducted the training after which the women were commissioned as second lieutenants. The training lasted fifteen months and included rocket technology, geophysics and navigational theory. Tereshkova learned to fly jets, experienced the effects of being spun on a centrifuge and spent time in an isolation chamber to simate the solitude of a space capsule.

Premier Nikita Khrushchev selected Tereshkova for the flight because she came from a family of collective workers, and this had value as a political symbol. Her flight was to be on Vostok 6, a dual flight to be in orbit at the same time with Vostok 5, which was launched two days earlier. Tereshkova was launched on June 16, 1963. She successfully ejected from her capsule and landed near Karanganda in Kazakhstan on June 19, 1963. Her flight consisted of 48 orbits for a total of 70 hours and 50 minutes in space.

After her historic flight, Tereshkova studied at Zhukovski Air Force Academy, graduating as a cosmonaut engineer in 1969. There have been speculations that Valentina trained for the Voskhod mission, which was to have a space-walk; but the flight did not take place. The female cosmonaut program was disbanded in 1969. The next space flight to have a woman was in 1982 when Svetlana Savitskaya flew on the Soyuz.

In 1976, Tereshkova earned a degree in technical sciences and was also awarded an honorary doctorate from the University of Edinburgh. She was awarded the Order of Lenin and Hero of the Soviet Union. She was chosen for several political positions due to her prominence. Tereshkova retired from the Air Force and the Cosmonaut Corps as a major general in 1997.

Tereshkova married cosmonaut Andrian Nikolayev in a public ceremony in November 1963 and they had one daughter, Yelena. The couple divorced in 1982. Tereshkova's second husband Dr. Juri Shaposhnikov, died in 1999. Tereshkova went on to earn high government positions in the Soviet Union up to the point of its collapse.

Although Tereshkova's flight has often been considered as only a Soviet publicity stunt for the space race between the U.S. and the Soviet Union, the flight benefited space exploration and furthered the involvement of women in space programs around the world.

Andrew Lloyd Webber

BIRTH NAME Andrew Lloyd Webber

BORN March 22, 1948

DROPPED OUT Oxford University

ANDREW LLOYD WEBBER was born in London into a musically inclined family. His father, William, was a composer and scholar of music at the Royal College of Music in London; and his mother, Jean, was a piano teacher. Andrew was fascinated with ancient musical instruments and played several instruments as a child, always preferring to play to his own compositions rather than those by other composers.

Andrew's aunt took him to his first musical on stage. From then on he was fascinated with musical theatre and began composing in earnest for plays in his school. He won a scholarship to study music at Magdalen College at Oxford University in 1964, but dropped out a year later to compose musicals with lyricist Tim Rice.

After a few unsuccessful pop songs and one musical, Webber and Rice had a success on their hands in 1968 with *Joseph and the Amazing Technicolor Dreamcoat,* a biblical-themed show with a rock and roll influence. The show was a hit in England as well as the U.S. In 1971, the two produced *Jesus Christ Superstar,* which was again a big hit. Webber wrote *Jeeves* with a new partner, Alan Ayckbourn; but the musical was not a success.

Webber again teamed with Rice for *Evita,* a musical based on the life of Eva Peron, wife of the Argentine dictator. The musical opened in 1978 in London and was a huge success. It was made into a movie, starring Madonna, by Alan Parker in 1996.

Webber wrote, *Cats* based on T.S. Eliot's poems in *Old Possum's Book of Practical Cats,* in 1981. The musical went on to become his most successful production. It was a hit for its simple plot, its backdrop of interesting costumes and junkyard set. *Cats* set the record for the longest running show in London and New York, where it closed after 7,485 performances, on September 10, 2000.

In 1984 Webber wrote a musical based on trains, *Starlight Express*. His next big hit came with *The Phantom of the Opera*, in 1986, which he wrote with Charles Hart and Richard Stilgoe. Several of Webber's later musicals, such as *Aspects of Love*, in 1989, *Sunset Boulevard*, in 1993, and *Whistle Down the Wind*, in 1997, were not as successful. Recent works include *Bombay Dreams*, in 2002, with Indian composer A.R. Rehman, and *The Woman in White*, in 2004.

Webber married Sarah Hugill in 1972 and they had two children, Imogen and Nicholas. After divorcing her in 1983, Webber married Sarah Brightman in 1984, with that marriage ending in divorce in 1991. The same year he married his third wife, Madeleine Gurdon, and they have three children, Alastair, William and Isabella.

Webber has won several awards over the years including seven Tony Awards, three Grammys, six Olivier Awards, a Golden Globe, an International Emmy and an Oscar. He was also awarded the Praemium Imperiale by the Japanese Art Association and the Richard Rodgers Award for Excellence in Musical Theatre. For his contribution to British music and theatre, Webber was knighted in 1992 and became an honorary life peer of the United Kingdom in 1997.

The most successful composer of modern times, Andrew Lloyd Webber broke the mold by being innovative, blending rock and roll, classical and operatic styles to create enchanting stage musicals. He is a true genius and master of his work, constantly blending different styles to make ever more innovative and grand productions.

Adolph Zukor

BIRTH NAME Adolph Zukor
BORN January 7, 1873
DIED June 10, 1976
DROPPED OUT High School

STUDIO MOGUL ADOLPH Zukor, who served as the president of Paramount Pictures until 1936, lived a rags-to-riches story worthy of a Hollywood movie. He revolutionized the movie industry by bringing film production, distribution and exhibition under one company.

Zukor was born in 1873, in Ricse, Hungary, which was then a part of the Austro-Hungarian Empire. His family had to struggle to make ends meet. He came to the U.S. when he was barely 16 and worked as a sweeper in a New York fur shop for a few years before he started his own fur shop in Chicago. In 1903, he purchased an amusement arcade. He then partnered up with dropout Marcus Loew and bought a chain of arcades, eventually becoming the treasurer of Marcus Loew's chain of movie theaters.

Zukor was innovative and a man of great vision. He saw a huge potential in the movie business and found a new strategy to attract crowds to theaters. He noticed that most Americans were reluctant to go to movie theaters. Zukor wanted to create a comfortable, magical and complete theatrical experience for moviegoers. His idea was to screen longer and more dramatic films. He started with the distribution of a four-reel European film, *Queen Elizabeth*. This proved to be a good beginning and he soon made enough profit to start the Famous Players Production Company. His company became known for bringing motion picture adaptations of popular Broadway shows to theaters. The company signed the famous actress Mary Pickford for its promotions and she remained associated with the company for years.

In 1916, Zukor merged his company with Jess L. Lasky Feature Play Company to form the Famous Players–Lasky Corporation. Five years later, he became its president. At that time, Paramount Distributions was a small company. Zukor purchased it and started buying movie theaters under the new name Paramount Pictures. In the years to come, Paramount Pictures became the biggest studio in Hollywood, with its strategy of integrating movie making and distribution.

Although Adolph Zukor was not actually involved with filmmaking, he managed the company's financial affairs from New York and the company did well till the 1930s, when it got into some financial problems. At that point, some people wanted Zukor out, but he stayed on. In 1935, Barney Balaban became Paramount's president. Zukor went on to become the company's chairman and remained so till 1976, when he died at the ripe age of 103.

Zukor's autobiography, *The Public is Never Wrong,* was published in 1953. He was successful because he understood what people wanted and also was a shrewd, hard-working and ambitious businessman. He was not born wealthy, but he created wealth with his great ideas and extraordinary vision.

$ **Millionaire Dropouts Trivia** **$**

Madame C.J. Walker, the first African-American millionaire, was a dropout.

Filmmakers

Filmmakers

Filmmakers

Filmmakers

Filmmakers

Filmmakers

Filmmakers

Filmmakers

Filmmakers

James Cameron

BIRTH NAME James Francis Cameron

BORN August 16, 1954

DROPPED OUT Fullerton College

JAMES CAMERON WAS born in Kapuskasing, Ontario. His father, Philip, was an electrical engineer and his mother, Shirley, was an artist. As a child James showed his propensity for leadership among his friends, instigating the building of go-carts, rockets and catapults. Encouraged by his mother, he painted, exhibiting his work at a local gallery. One of his earliest inspirations was the film, *2001: A Space Odyssey*. He began to experiment with filmmaking and photographed the model space ships he built.

The family moved to Fullerton, California, in 1971. Cameron enrolled in Fullerton College, majoring in physics and later in English, eventually dropping out of college, as he was unable to decide if he should focus on art or science. *Star Wars* rekindled his fascination with film production and he decided to study on his own terms, using the resources of the library of the University of Southern California to study special effects technology, optical printing and projection techniques.

Cameron's first job was at the Roger Corman Studios as a miniature model maker. He progressed to become an art director for the sci-fi movie *Battle Beyond the Stars* and also worked on *Escape from New York*. His big break came in 1981 when he was chosen by Italian producer Ovidio G. Assonitis to make *Piranha Part Two: The Spawning*. Assonitis had selected Cameron to save money and to have full control over the movie, but Cameron wanted to have creative license and the two fought constantly. The movie was underfinanced and had an Italian crew who knew no English; it ended up being a disaster.

Cameron was constantly under stress because the low quality of his work. He had a nightmare about an invisible robot hit man sent from the future to kill him—the birth of the *Terminator* series. As he wanted to direct the film himself, Cameron was rejected by the major studios. He eventually made a deal with producer Gale Anne Hurd, selling her the movie rights for one dollar. It was his unending enthusiasm and passion that convinced Arnold Schwarzenegger to star in the film. *The Terminator* was a huge success and paved Cameron's way in Hollywood, establishing his reputation as a screenwriter and director.

Cameron wrote the screenplays of *Rambo: First Blood Part 2* and *Aliens* while waiting for *The Terminator* to be financed. With the film's success, he was asked to direct *Aliens*, which won Oscars for best visual effects and best sound effects. In the following years Cameron made action films including *The Abyss, Point Break, Terminator 2: Judgment Day* and *True Lies*.

Cameron surprised everyone by selecting a love story set on the doomed ocean liner *Titanic* as his next film. After a grueling schedule that was millions of dollars over budget, the movie created history by breaking box office records the world over. It became the top grossing film of all time. Starring Leonardo DiCaprio and Kate Winslet, the movie won eleven Academy Awards, including best director and best picture.

Cameron's single-minded focus on films has led to upheavals in his private life. He has been married five times, to Sharon Williams, producer Gale Anne Hurd, director Katherine Bigelow, *Terminator* star Linda Hamilton and Suzy Amis.

James Cameron has succeeded in Hollywood on his own terms, creating his art with a passion few possess and at a high personal cost. He never learned to accept defeat, always finding a way to succeed. He believes in creating his own destiny, never taking 'no' for an answer.

Peter Jackson

BIRTH NAME Peter Jackson

BORN October 31, 1961

DROPPED OUT High School

PETER JACKSON WAS born in Wellington and grew up in the neighboring town of Pukerua Bay in New Zealand. As an only child, he developed a vivid imagination and gave free rein to it when his parents received an 8 mm camera as a gift in 1969. Mastering camera techniques, Peter began making movies with it, dropping out of high school and getting a job at the local newspaper. Born on Halloween, he became fascinated with horror movies after seeing films such as *Evil Dead* and *Dawn of the Dead*.

Working as a cinematographer for various TV shows in New Zealand from the age of seventeen, Jackson made his directorial debut with *Roast of the Day*, in 1983, a ten-minute short that was later expanded to a feature-length movie, *Bad Taste*. The movie became a cult classic and set the tone for Jackson's style of cinema, full of blood, guts and gore. His next film was *Meet the Feebles*, a story about a group of puppets and their television show, which again was a feast of twisted humor, graphic violence and Jackson's trademark blood and guts scenes.

Jackson's next film, *Brain Dead*, re-titled *Dead Alive* for U.S. audiences, was named by the New York *Daily News* as "the goriest fright film of all time." The movie surpassed his earlier movies, showing an unending stream of blood and severed limbs. With each of his first three films, he earned appreciation among cultists and became firmly entrenched as the king of gore.

In 1994, Jackson made *Heavenly Creatures*, starring Kate Winslet, a true story about two schoolgirls who murdered one's mother. The movie was well received and won several honors, including the Silver Lion at the Venice Film Festival. His next few movies, *The Frighteners*, starring Michael J. Fox, *Forgotten Silver*, a black and white film narrated by Sam Neill and *Jack Brown, Genius,* based on the life of historically neglected New Zealand filmmaker Colin McKenzie, were all commercially and critically disappointing.

Jackson started his most ambitious plan in 1998, adapting J.R.R. Tolkien's famous trilogy *Lord of the Rings,* for which he selected a large and talented cast. The first film, *Lord of the Rings: The Fellowship of the Ring,* was a huge success; it received thirteen Oscar nominations and won for best cinematography, best visual effects, best makeup and best score. The second movie, *The Lord of the Rings: The Two Towers,* was an even bigger commercial success and received six Oscar nominations, winning for best sound editing and best visual effects. The third movie, *The Lord of the Rings: The Return of the King,* again opened to rave reviews and huge commercial success and went on to win all eleven Oscars it had been nominated for, tying with *Ben-Hur* and *Titanic* for the most Oscars won by a single film.

Instead of moving to Hollywood, Jackson makes his movies in his native New Zealand, which has led to great deal of business in Miramar to support his film production. Taking advantage of the time difference between New Zealand and the U.S., Jackson provides digital special effects to several Hollywood films via telecommunication and satellite links.

Peter Jackson is fiercely independent, famously offbeat and a perfectionist. He is one of the few horror movie directors to have bridged the gap to mainstream cinema and is respected for his intense dedication on *Lord of the Rings.* He has a large cult following for his gory style of cinema.

Michael Moore

BIRTH NAME Michael Moore
BORN April 23, 1954
DROPPED OUT University of Michigan–Flint

MICHAEL MOORE WAS born in Davison, Michigan. Both his father and grandfather worked at the local General Motors plant and lost their jobs when GM closed the factory. These issues played an important part in shaping Moore's passion for revealing corporate injustice and greed.

In high school, Moore created a slide show that exposed environmentally unfriendly businesses, setting the tone for future projects. He became one of the youngest people elected to public office when he won a seat on the Flint School Board in 1972, when he was 18. Enrolling at the University of Michigan–Flint, Moore dropped out soon after to focus on activism and started working at a local newspaper, *The Flint Voice*. Soon becoming the editor, he expanded the paper to cover the entire Midwest. He then joined *Mother Jones* magazine as editor, but his confrontational style led to his being fired in less than a year.

Moore worked briefly for a Ralph Nader organization and then decided to make a film about his hometown, Flint, and the impact of the closure of General Motors automobile plants on the local economy. The result, *Roger & Me* was one of the most commercially successful documentary films ever made and received honors at several film festivals. He followed up with *Pets or Meat: The Return to Flint*, a half-hour television film that was a continuation of *Roger & Me*.

Moore's first fictional film was *Canadian Bacon*, a black comedy starring John Candy, who died soon after. Moore then produced a satiric news and commentary show called *TV Nation*, a summer replacement show that attracted a small fan base but lasted only two seasons. Moore produced another television show, *The Awful Truth*, a mix of comedy and political commentary. It aired in 1999 and 2000.

Moore published a book, *Downsize This!: Random Threats From an Unarmed American*, which became a bestseller. While he traveled across the U.S. promoting the book, Moore made a documentary titled, *The Big One*, capturing economic inequality in the country. His next book, *Stupid White Men*, was published in early 2002 and was a major bestseller. The book openly criticized George W. Bush.

Increasingly in the media spotlight for his controversial opinions, Moore became widely known. His next film, *Bowling for Columbine*, delved into the country's fascination with guns and violence. It was featured at the Cannes Film Festival, where it received the Jury Award. The film also won the 2002 Oscar for best documentary

Moore's most famous and controversial film was *Fahrenheit 9/11*, a hard-hitting look at the Bush administration's ties to Osama bin Laden's family and the Bush family's ulterior motives for going to war. The film won the Palm D'Or at the Cannes Film Festival in 2004 and was both a commercial and critical success.

Michael Moore uses his trademark wit and caustic humor to report on injustice and malfeasance. As a fearless investigator of and commentator on political and economic attitudes in America, he has carved out a place for himself as an iconoclast, gadfly and defender of the common man.

$ **Millionaire Dropouts Trivia** $

One of the top-grossing films of 2005, War of the Worlds, was written by a dropout (H.G. Wells), was directed by a dropout (Steven Spielberg) and starred a dropout (Tom Cruise).

Kevin Smith

BIRTH NAME Kevin Patrick Smith
BORN August 2, 1970
DROPPED OUT New School for Social Research

KEVIN SMITH GREW up in Highlands, New Jersey. After graduating from high school, he enrolled in the New School for Social Research for a program in creative writing, soon dropping out. He entered the Vancouver Film School but soon dropped out from there, too, and returned to New Jersey to work at a convenience store.

Smith's experiences at the store, combined with seeing the low-budget hit *Slackers,* inspired him to write the script for *Clerks.* He and co-producer Scott Mosier, a friend from the Vancouver Film School, financed the movie by collecting $27,000 from parents, loans and the sale of Smith's comic book collection. They also employed friends and local actors for the film and used the same convenience store as a set, filming at night and working behind the counter during the day. The movie made its debut at the Sundance Film Festival in 1994 to good reviews and soon became a mascot of independent movies, as it demonstrated the ability of making movies on a low budget.

Smith's next venture, *Mallrats,* which he wrote in 1995, narrates the difficulties in the romantic life of two slackers, who spend most of their time at a mall. The movie starred Shannen Doherty of *Beverly Hills 90210* fame, Ben Affleck, Jason Lee and Jeremy London, but was a failure with the critics as well as general audiences. In 1997, Smith made *Chasing Amy,* a movie about love and loss that surprised critics with its emotional depth and fared moderately at the box office. *Clerks, Mallrats* and *Chasing Amy* were all set and filmed in New Jersey.

In 1999, Smith made *Dogma,* a controversial movie that religious groups claimed was blasphemous and that led to several protests. In 2001, he made *Jay and Silent Bob Strike Back* with his recurring characters; it had a huge list of cameo appearances. He also wrote scripts for comic books Daredevil and Green Arrow.

After gaining recognition for his films, Smith traveled to colleges across the country, conducting question and answer sessions on his personal style of filmmaking. He eventually taped two sessions and compiled a DVD, called *An Evening with Kevin Smith*, which was such a success that he decided to make another DVD from sessions in Toronto and London.

His next two movies *Jersey Girl* and *Gigli*, both had Ben Affleck and Jennifer Lopez in them. They did not do well, as the films were overshadowed by the media attention on the actors' off-screen relationship.

In 2006, Smith reconnected with his slacker past and filmed *Clerks II*, with the original characters now more than a decade older.

Smith is married to Jennifer Schwalbach, whom he met when she interviewed him for *USA Today*. They have a daughter, Harley Quinn, named after a character in *Batman*. Smith received an honorary doctorate from Montclair State University in 2004 and another honorary degree from the Vancouver Film School in 2005.

Smith bought back his comics collection after the success of *Clerks* and opened a comic book store, Jay and Silent Bob's Secret Stash, in Red Bank, New Jersey. He owns his own production company, View Askew, and makes short films for *The Tonight Show with Jay Leno*. Smith is known for his unique style of mixing bold, colorful characters and raunchy dialogues with a keen perception of American culture.

Kevin Smith is one of the directors who brought independent film making to the mainstream in the 1990s. With his keen sense of picking up the undercurrents of popular culture, he carved a niche for himself in the independent film industry.

John Woo

BIRTH NAME John Woo

BORN May 1, 1946

DROPPED OUT High School

JOHN WOO WAS born in Guangzhou, China. His family moved to Hong Kong when he was five, because of persecution for their Christian background. The family had a difficult time in Hong Kong, as John's father suffered from tuberculosis and could not work; they became homeless when their house burned down. John's mother introduced him to films, his early favorites being American musicals. His favorite movie from that time, *The Wizard of Oz*, remains close to his heart.

Woo witnessed a high crime level when he lived in Hong Kong. This affected him deeply. He went to the movie theatres to escape and learned that there was more to this world than just violence and suffering. His father died when Woo was 16. He dropped out of school to work at a newspaper, *The Chinese Student Weekly*, and learned about films by stealing books from local bookstores and libraries.

Woo's first job in the movie industry, when he was 23, was as a script supervisor at Cathay Studios. In a few years he became an assistant director at Shaw Studios, with Chang Cheh guiding him. In 1974, Woo directed his first movie, *The Young Dragons*, choreographed by Jackie Chan.

Through most of the 1980s and 1990s, Woo made numerous action comedies, none of which were successful. He was reaching burnout stage and decided to move to Taiwan to take a break. His career really took off with *A Better Tomorrow*, a movie that captured all the ingredients to make a successful John Woo film, with drama, slow-motion action scenes and a tough, gritty backdrop.

Woo made several movies with actor Chow Yun-Fat, in his trademark gangster style, depicting men of honor who have become out-casts in a greedy world. The movie that brought him international recognition was *The Killer*, which has been called as the best Hong Kong movie ever made and made Woo a cult favorite. Moving to the U.S. when Hong Kong was handed over to China in 1997, Woo found that the studios in Hollywood placed a number of restrictions on his directorial freedom and that the rating system curtailed his creativity.

The first Hollywood film Woo made was *Hard Target*, with Jean Claude Van Damme. After three years he made *Broken Arrow*, with John Travolta and Christian Slater. Although both movies were fast-paced and action-packed, they did not have his trademark style of combining emotion and drama along with the requisite action.

Woo was finally given the freedom to make a film his way with *Face/Off*, a script he had rejected many times earlier. The movie, starring John Travolta and Nicholas Cage, opened to commercial and critical acclaim. In one stroke, Woo had become part of an elite group of top-league Hollywood directors.

In subsequent years, Woo made the super-successful *Mission: Impossible II* along with disappointing films like *Windtalkers* and *Paycheck*, which had little emotion, drama and action.

John Woo is the first Asian director to make his mark in the top league in Hollywood. His trademark style of blending emotional drama with action scenes shot in slow motion has earned him cult status. Although several critics have written him off after his recent failures, Woo is a fighter and has built a loyal fan base for his particular brand of cinema. He has created his own style with his elaborate action sequences, ballet-like violence and themes of honor and loyalty.

Comedians

Comedians

Comedians

Comedians

Comedians

Comedians

Comedians

Comedians

Comedians

Carol Burnett

BIRTH NAME Carol Creighton Burnett
BORN April 26, 1936
DROPPED OUT University of California, Los Angeles

"WHEN YOU HAVE a dream, you've got to grab it and never let go." Carol Burnett followed her dream and became one of the best-loved comedians in America. An accomplished actress, singer and dancer, she always had the knack of connecting with audiences.

Burnett was born in San Antonio, Texas. Her parents, Jodie and Louise Burnett, were both alcoholics, Carol's grandmother in Los Angeles raised her. Carol's father died in 1954 of tuberculosis and pneumonia and her mother died in 1957. Burnett graduated from Hollywood High School and enrolled in UCLA, eventually dropping out as she got increasingly better parts on TV.

Burnett was first noticed in the mid-1950s when she sang "I Made a Fool of Myself over John Foster Dulles." She also acted with Buddy Hackett in *Stanley*, a TV show on NBC that lasted only one season. In 1959, she drew praise for her performance in the Broadway musical *Once Upon a Mattress*. Her role as a cleaning lady on *The Garry Moore Show* lasted longer, though, until 1962, establishing her popularity with the national television audience and leading to a special with Julie Andrews, *Julie and Carol at Carnegie Hall*, in 1962.

Burnett was a panelist on the TV game show *Password*, appearing until the early 1980s. But she is most famous for her own show, *The Carol Burnett Show*, which ran from 1967 to 1978 and won 22 Emmy Awards. The show is still in syndication. Burnett's hallmarks, her expressive face and deep-throated voice, suited her to a variety of comic roles.

Burnett also gained fame in legal circles. She successfully sued the *National Enquirer* in 1981 for libel, when the tabloid wrote about her alleged drunkenness in public with Henry Kissinger. It was a sensitive issue for Carol as both her parents had suffered from alcoholism. The case is seen as a landmark in libel cases by celebrities against tabloid journalists.

Burnett acted in movies, too, including *The Four Seasons, Annie, Pete 'n' Tillie* and *Noises Off,* returning to TV in the hit sitcom *Mad About You,* in a supporting role as Jamie Buchman's mother. She also appeared in her favorite soap opera, *All My Children,* as Verla Grubbs, a role that was created especially for her. For a short time in 1991, she returned to television with a new show, *Carol and Company.*

Burnett married Don Saroyan on December 15, 1955, and divorced him in 1962, to marry Joe Hamilton in 1963. With him she had three daughters, Carrie, Jody and Erin. Carrie, a talented actress, died of lung cancer in 2002. Burnett has been married to Brian Miller since 2001.

Burnett has received several awards over the years. In 1963, she was awarded the Peabody. She won five Emmy Awards, eight Golden Globe Awards and in 2003 received the Kennedy Center Honors. Carol Burnett has endeared herself to millions of Americans. She loves the art of performing more than the fame she has received from it. In her words, "Celebrity was a long time in coming; it will go away. Everything goes away."

Bill Cosby

BIRTH NAME William Henry Cosby, Jr.

BORN July 12, 1937

DROPPED OUT Temple University

BILL COSBY WAS born in Philadelphia, Pennsylvania. His father, William Cosby, Sr., was a mess steward in the U.S. Navy. His mother, Anna Cosby, earned eight dollars a day working as a maid. Bill Cosby's childhood was fraught with difficulty. He had to drop out of high school when he was in his tenth grade to join the Navy. He completed high school through correspondence and earned an scholarship in the field of athletics at Temple University. Realizing that he had the ability to make people laugh, he abandoned his plans to teach athletics and worked hard to become a comedian.

Cosby supported himself as a bartender for many years. He became a nightclub comedian, recounting incidents from his childhood and making people laugh. He appeared on prime time television shows, including *The Tonight Show with Johnny Carson*. He won two Emmy awards for his portrayal of a wisecracking spy in the adventure show *I Spy*. He played the role of a gym teacher in *The Bill Cosby Show*. He sold several Grammy Award–winning comedy albums in the 1960s. He won a Grammy every year from 1965 to 1970. He won again in 1987. By 2005, he had earned three gold and six platinum comedy albums. His television shows included *The New Bill Cosby Show, Fat Albert and the Cosby Kids, The Cosby Show* and *The Cosby Mysteries*.

Although Cosby's movie career did not take off as well as his comedy career, he did star in a few successful movies, including *Uptown Saturday Night*, with Sydney Poitier; *Let's Do it Again*, with Raquel Welch and Harvey Keitel; and *A Piece of the Action*, a Sydney Poitier production. He also acted in a few less successful films.

The Cosby Show was a huge success. Cosby can be counted among the highest-paid comedians and one of the wealthiest entertainers in U.S. entertainment history. Although he was famous and wealthy, Cosby went back to school and earned a doctorate in education from the University of Massachusetts in 1977. As an educator, he tried to integrate teaching with television using television programs to promote awareness of social issues like illiteracy, drug abuse, teenage pregnancies and gang violence. He also hosted the popular television program *Kids Say the Darndest Things*. His album *Cosby Talks to Kids* urged kids not to get involved with drugs.

Cosby's 27-year-old son Ennis, a doctoral student at Columbia University, was shot at and killed when he was changing the tires of his Mercedes on a Los Angeles freeway. Mikhail Markhasev, the killer, is serving a life sentence as a result of Cosby's speaking against giving him the death penalty.

Cosby received the Kennedy Center Honors award in 1998 and the Presidential Medal of Freedom in 2002. In 2005, when a poll was conducted in Britain to pick "The Comedian's Comedian," he was voted among the top 50 comedy acts ever by fellow comedians and comedy insiders.

Cosby has provided celebrity endorsements for various big companies. He was linked so closely with Jell-O that he collected his payment in part ownership of the company that makes it. From his humble childhood days, Bill Cosby has indeed come a long way with hard work and determination.

Ellen DeGeneres

BIRTH NAME Ellen Lee DeGeneres

BORN January 26, 1958

DROPPED OUT University of New Orleans

E LLEN DEGENERES WAS born in Metairie, Louisiana. Her father, Elliot, an insurance salesman, and her mother, Betty, a
real estate agent, divorced when Ellen was 13. Ellen and her mother
moved from New Orleans to Atlanta, Texas.

On graduation from high school in 1976, DeGeneres enrolled at
the University of New Orleans to major in communications. She
dropped out after a semester and worked at several jobs including
selling vacuum cleaners door-to-door, shucking oysters, bartending,
and doing clerical work for a law firm. In the meantime she started
performing a stand-up comedy routine, first at friends' parties and
then at clubs around New Orleans, finally taking a job as the emcee
at Clyde's Comedy Club.

In 1982, HBO ran a national contest to find the funniest person in
America. DeGeneres won the contest in New Orleans and went on
to win statewide in Louisiana and finally came out on top in the national contest. This led to performances on late night talk and comedy shows, including, in 1986, *The Tonight Show with Johnny Carson.*

DeGeneres got her feet wet in television with appearances in *Open
House* and *Laurie Hill* during the 1989–1990 season. She got her own
show, *These Friends of Mine,* later renamed *Ellen,* in 1994. The show
lasted till 1998 and was a runaway success, topping the ratings and
winning DeGeneres two Emmy Awards. On the show, she came
out as a lesbian in 1997. While that did not hurt the show's ratings,
the shift in focus to her character's relationships eventually bored
the audience. After the show was canceled, DeGeneres returned to
stand-up comedy. Her next television show, *The Ellen Show,* ran on
CBS for the 2001–2002 season.

DeGeneres also did two hugely successful stand-up comedy routines shown on HBO, *The Beginning* and *Here and Now*, in addition to hosting The Grammy Awards, Emmy Awards, VH1 Honors and the *Saturday Night Live Christmas Special*.

DeGeneres's first movie role was a small part in *Coneheads* in 1993, and her first lead role came in the romantic comedy *Mr. Wrong* in 1996. Other movies she has acted in include *Goodbye Lover*, *Edtv* and *If These Walls Could Talk 2*. She also did the voiceover for Dory in the animated movie *Finding Nemo*.

DeGeneres launched her own talk show, *The Ellen DeGeneres Show*, in 2003. The show has risen consistently in the ratings, outlasting several other talk shows that started around the same time. The show has received eleven nominations for Daytime Emmy Awards and in its first year won four awards.

DeGeneres's book *My Point...And I Do Have One*, published in 1996, topped the *New York Times* bestseller list. Her second book *The Funny Thing Is...*, consisting of short stories and essays, was also successful.

Ellen DeGeneres has created a brand of comedy entirely her own, narrating stories using bizarre word associations while maintaining a naïve expression. She has often been called a female Seinfeld, for her ability to turn the mundane into something outrageously funny.

Kevin James

BIRTH NAME Kevin George Knipfing
BORN April 26, 1965
DROPPED OUT Cortland University

COMEDIAN KEVIN JAMES of *The King of Queens* is known for his comic timing and deadpan dialogue delivery style. Born as Kevin George Knipfing in Mineola, New York, Kevin grew up in Stony Brook, New York. Kevin's father, Joe, is an insurance broker, and his mother, Janet, is a homemaker. Kevin has one older brother, Gary, and one younger sister, Leslie.

James attended Ward Melville High School in Long Island. On graduating in 1983 Kevin enrolled in Cortland University, where he majored in sports management and was a fullback on the university football team. After three years of college, James dropped out and joined a community theatre in the summer. The audience reaction to his comic performance led him to decide to focus on a career in comedy. He joined the improvisation group started by his brother, Gary Valentine.

James spent eleven years performing stand-up comedy in clubs. Things started looking up when he participated in Star Search in 1983. In 1992 appeared on *The Tonight Show with Jay Leno*. His winning the Just for Laughs Montreal Comedy Festival in 1996 was his breakthrough into the comedy and acting worlds.

Ray Romano, a close friend from James's days as a stand-up comedian, got him a job as a writer on Romano's show, *Everybody Loves Raymond,* and soon James had written a recurring role for himself into the sitcom—playing himself—in 1997 and 1998. He convinced network executives to give him his own sitcom, *The King of Queens,* in 1998 on CBS. In the show, James plays the lead role of a hardworking delivery truck driver, representing the average working class Joe. Leah Remini plays his wife and Jerry Stiller plays his father-in-law. James's brother Gary also has a part on the show as his cousin Danny.

James starred in *Sweat the Small Stuff*, on Comedy Central, in 2001, and still tours in the U.S. when *The King of Queens* is not shooting, performing stand-up comedy. He was selected by Will Smith, who is a big fan of *The King of Queens*, for a part in the romantic comedy Hitch. James has gone on to additional film roles, as well.

James was inspired by fellow New Yorkers and comics like Jerry Seinfeld and Robert Klein. Besides acting, James is also an executive producer on *The King of Queens*. *Entertainment Weekly* included James in their list of the 100 most creative people in entertainment in 2000. With fame and recognition have come numerous appearances on *The Late Show with David Letterman* and guest roles in several sitcoms, including *Becker* and *Martial Law*.

James is a sports lover. He is an accomplished golfer, a fan of his home teams, the New York Jets and the New York Mets, and a fan of the Ultimate Fighting Championship. He is married to model Steffiana De La Cruz, whom he met on a blind date in 2000. Their first child, Sienna Marie, was born in 2005.

Although focused on *The King of Queens*, James keeps in touch with all forms of comedy, touring the country and performing at clubs and on shows. His upbeat and positive attitude, quick repartee and connection with the common man have made him a star.

Rosie O'Donnell

BIRTH NAME Roseanne Teresa O'Donnell

BORN March 21, 1962

DROPPED OUT Dickinson College
and Boston University

ROSIE O'DONNELL WAS born in Commack, New York, on Long Island. Her father, Edward, worked for a defense corporation as a spy camera engineer. Her mother, Roseanne, died when she was 10. Rosie attended Commack High School.

O'Donnell studied for a short time at Dickinson College and at Boston University but dropped out to pursue an acting career, initially doing stand-up comedy. Her break came when she was cast as Maggie O'Brien in the sitcom Gimme a Break, where she stood out because of her tomboyish appearance and New York accent. In the late 1980s, O'Donnell produced and also hosted *Stand-Up Spotlight*, a stand-up series on VH-1. She got her own show, *Stand By Your Man*, in 1992; but it was soon canceled.

Her success grew with appearances in hit films *A League of Their Own*, *Another Stakeout* and *Sleepless in Seattle* and in critically acclaimed films like *Now and Then*, *Beautiful Girls* and the children's movie *Harriet the Spy*. But a few movies like *Car 54: Where are you?* and *Exit to Eden* did not fare well commercially.

O'Donnell got her own daytime talk show, *The Rosie O'Donnell Show*, in 1996. The show focused on lighthearted entertainment instead of serious issues, often raising money for charitable projects. The show did well and O'Donnell won Daytime Emmy Awards for Outstanding Talk Show Host from 1997 to 1999.

O'Donnell partnered with *McCall's* in 2000 to produce a new magazine, *Rosie's McCall's*, focused on real women and real issues, such as depression, breast cancer and foster care. The magazine was unable to attract enough advertisers and soon folded.

In 2002, before retiring from her talk show, O'Donnell announced she was a lesbian. She returned to stand-up comedy and changed her image drastically from sweet to brash and abrasive. Her shows often made fun of prominent celebrities.

Find Me, O'Donnell's autobiography, was published in 2002. The book received critical praise and rose to the number two spot on the *New York Times* bestseller list. O'Donnell married Kelli Carpenter in 2004; two weeks after the mayor of San Francisco started allowing same-sex marriages in the city.

In 2005, O'Donnell returned to acting and produced *Riding the Bus with My Sister*, in which she played the role of a mentally retarded girl. She won critical praise for it and was short-listed for the 2006 Emmy Award nominations.

Rosie O'Donnell's upbeat and cheerful image has endeared her to millions of Americans. She is a comedian, actress and talk show host known for her quick-witted and aggressive humor. She is fearlessly outspoken and passionate about the causes she believes in.

Keenan Ivory Wayans

BIRTH NAME Keenan Ivory Wayans

BORN June 8, 1958

DROPPED OUT Tuskegee University

KEENAN IVORY WAYANS acted in and directed *In Living Color,* a wild and crazy comedy show on Fox TV that not only made him famous but was also the launching pad for several other comedians. At its peak, the show was favorably compared to *Saturday Night Live.*

Keenan Ivory Wayans was born in New York City into a large family. Keenan's father, Howell, worked as a supermarket manager; and his mother, Elvira, was a social worker. Keenan has five sisters and four brothers, Damon, Dwayne, Marlon and Shawn, who have often appeared with him. Keenan graduated from Seward Park High School in 1976 and entered Tuskegee University in Alabama on an engineering scholarship. He dropped out in his senior year to focus on a career in stand-up comedy.

Wayans, being only modestly successful as a stand-up comedian in New York, moved to Los Angeles to try his hand at movies and television. He appeared in *Tinseltown,* a quirky comedy depicting the struggle of a black man in Hollywood, strikingly similar to his own experiences.

Wayans also played a customer in the hit sitcom *Cheers* and briefly had a recurring role in *For Love and Honor,* a military-based soap opera in 1983. He co-wrote and appeared on *Raw,* Eddie Murphy's concert classic. (He had met Eddie Murphy during his stand-up comedian days and had always been a Murphy fan.)

Wayans did not restrict himself to acting. He wrote, directed and acted in a spoof called *I'm Gonna Get You Sucka,* which Fox TV executives noticed even though it was not a commercial success.

In 1990 Fox gave Wayans a shot at writing and producing his

own show. *In Living Color* was a wild, wacky, no-holds-barred and mostly black comedy. The show was a hit and Keenan Ivory Wayans became famous. The show also brought fame to several of his brothers and upcoming stars like Jim Carrey, Jamie Foxx and David Allen Grier.

Wayans had a dispute with network executives and left the show after two years to focus on movies. He wrote and directed a comedy, *A Low Down Dirty Shame*, in 1994; but it did not do well. His next ventures were action films *The Glimmer Man* in 1996 and *Most Wanted* in 1997, which he wrote. Again they did not set the box office on fire. Disillusioned with his unsuccessful run in Hollywood, he decided to start his own late-night talk show, *The Keenan Ivory Wayans Show*.

Although he has done a few cameos and a guest role on his brother Damon's *My Wife and Kids*, Keenan Wayans is not focusing on an acting career. In 2000, he directed *Scary Movie*, a spoof of horror movies. It was a big hit and led to two sequels. Wayans also directed and co-wrote *White Chicks*, in which his brothers Marlon and Shawn starred.

Wayans has attributed his success to Richard Pryor. He said, "I just dreamed about being like Richard Pryor. Pryor started it all. He's Yoda. If Pryor had not come along, there would not be an Eddie Murphy or a Keenen Ivory Wayans or a Damon Wayans or an Arsenio Hall—or even a [white comedian like] Sam Kinison, for that matter. He made the blueprint for the progressive thinking of black comedians, unlocked that irreverent style."

Actors

Nicolas Cage

BIRTH NAME Nicholas Kim Coppola
BORN January 7, 1964
DROPPED OUT Beverly Hills High School

OSCAR WINNING ACTOR Nicolas Cage always wanted to make it big on his own. He belonged to a family of achievers. His father August Coppola was a professor; his mother Joy Vogelsang, a famous dancer and choreographer; his uncle was Francis Ford Coppola, the director of *The Godfather*. Nicolas did not want to ride on the fame of his uncle or his family and dreamt of making a name for himself on his own merit.

Nicholas was born in the busy seaport city of Long Beach, California. His parents separated when he was barely 12. His father then moved with him to Beverly Hills. It was here that he was exposed to films, literature and other artistic influences. He entered Beverly Hills High School to study acting but soon dropped out to focus on honing his acting skills. He had already appeared in a TV show while still in school and felt that actual acting experience was much more valuable than any academic qualification.

Nicholas's first break came when he acted in *Fast Times at Ridgemont High*, Cameron Crowe's first movie. His role in the movie was cut drastically. Disappointed, he took to selling popcorn at the Fairfax Theater. He hoped that this would in some way take him closer to movies and maybe acting. He soon got a chance to act in his uncle's *Valley Girl*, where he used his stage name Nicolas Cage for the first time instead of his real name Nicholas Coppola. He took the name Cage, as he was a great admirer of the comic book hero Luke Cage. He couldn't help feeling that the Coppola name made people look at him differently. He felt he would not be recognized for what he actually was. Always wanting to succeed on his own

150   www.MillionaireDropouts.com

terms, the change in name enabled him to achieve what he wanted without any stigmas attached.

Cage is passionate about his craft. He studied Method acting, doing a lot of research and living out his roles. For his role as a gangster in *The Cotton Club*, he is reported to have smashed a street vendor's remote-control car to get a feel of the anger and the sense of rage of a gangster. In the movie *Peggy Sue Got Married*, he was criticized for his intense desire to live the role by speaking in a strange voice and wearing weird teeth.

Cher took notice of Cage and asked him to star opposite her in *Moonstruck*. He played the role with such intensity that he was nominated for a Golden Globe award. In *Vampire's Kiss*, he was supposed to eat a raw egg, according to the script, but decided to eat a live cockroach instead, for better effect. For his role in *Birdy*, he had a tooth extracted without anesthesia to feel the actual pain that an injured soldier suffers. Such is his passion for acting.

A huge fan of Elvis Presley, Cage acted as a thug in *Wild at Heart* and sang "Love Me Tender" for the movie. In *Honeymoon in Vegas*, he played an Elvis impersonator. He was also married to Presley's daughter, Lisa Marie Presley, for a brief period.

In 1995, he won a best actor Oscar for *Leaving Las Vegas*, where he played the role of an alcoholic who, after losing his job, moves to Las Vegas and drinks himself to death. His performance in the movie also fetched him the Golden Globe award for best actor.

Cage is married to Alice Kim and lives in the outskirts of Los Angles. Known for his intense portrayal of any character he plays, Nicolas Cage has overcome the attachment to his famous roots and has gone on to be a major star in his own right.

Jim Carrey

BIRTH NAME James Eugene Carrey

BORN January 17, 1962

DROPPED OUT Agincourt Collegiate Institute

JIM CARREY IS a top Hollywood actor famous for his hilarious, rubber-faced antics and endless energy. He has entertained audiences the world over with his comic acting in *The Mask, Liar Liar* and many other movies. Although he has succeeded in making the world laugh with him, his real life story, especially his childhood days, has little to laugh about.

Jim Carrey was born in Newmarket, Ontario, Canada. His father, Percy, was an accountant. Jim was the youngest of four children. He loved to perform and entertain people. At Aldershot High School he performed stand-up comedy acts for his classmates. He watched TV shows, keenly observed different actors and their styles and later practiced impersonating them in the basement. He wore his tap shoes to bed, just in case his parents needed some cheering up in the middle of the night.

The Carrey family fell into hard times when Percy lost his job. Jim was in the ninth grade. The family was forced to move to Scarborough from Newmarket and all of them had to work at the Titan Wheels factory. Jim worked an eight-hour shift every day after school. When the family finally quit the factory, they lived in a Volkswagen camper van for a while before moving to Toronto.

Carrey's first attempt to break into the comedy scene was a disaster. He performed at Yuk Yuk's, a local club, and the show did not do well. Disappointed, he spent the next two years improvising and reworking his material. When he performed again, he was a major hit.

He dropped out of high school and moved to Los Angeles in 1979. One story Carrey loves to tell everyone is how he celebrated his arrival in Hollywood in his old Toyota and with no work at hand. He wrote himself a post-dated check for ten million dollars and kept it with him as a source of inspiration. Work was not hard to come by, though. He performed at the Comedy Store and was noticed by the veteran comic Rodney Dangerfield, who hired him for an entire season. He also played the role of a cartoonist in the sitcom *Duck Factory*.

Carrey's first film was as a male lead in *Once Bitten*, 1985. He went on to act in moderately successful films like *Peggy Sue Got Married* and *Earth Girls Are Easy*. He then played the role of psychotic Fire Marshall Bill in the comedy show *In Living Color*, 1990. He returned to the big screen in 1994 with *Ace Ventura: Pet Detective*, which banked entirely on Carrey's physical humor. Then he starred in *The Mask* with Cameron Diaz and *Dumb and Dumber* with Jeff Daniels. Both movies did well at the box office. Just three days before his father's death, Carrey received $10 million dollars for *The Mask*. He slipped the old check he had written to himself into his dad's pocket before the coffin was closed.

In 1996, Carrey played a disturbed loner in *The Cable Guy*. The film did not do well, but he bounced back a year later with *Liar, Liar.* He moved on to a different genre with *The Truman Show*, 1998, for which he won the Golden Globe for best actor. His brilliant performance in *Man on the Moon*, 1991, earned him another Golden Globe. He went on to star in *Eternal Sunshine of the Spotless Mind, Bruce Almighty* and *How the Grinch Stole Christmas.*

Jim Carrey is a brilliant actor who can send anyone into peals of laughter at the drop of a hat. He has won the hearts of millions of fans for both his on-screen performance and his success in real life—a life filled with hardship in his youth.

Sean Connery

BIRTH NAME Thomas Connery
BORN August 25, 1930
DROPPED OUT High School

SIIR THOMAS SEAN Connery was born in Edinburgh, Scotland, to a working class family. He worked hard even as a small boy, delivering newspapers and milk. When he was 13, he dropped out of school. A few years later, he signed up with the Royal Navy for seven years, but after a two-year stint he was discharged when he was diagnosed with peptic ulcers. Connery continued to do odd jobs to support himself. He worked in the steel mills, he delivered coal and he even learned French polishing.

Connery was drawn towards bodybuilding. He participated in a Mr. Universe competition and began to pose for photo shoots. He was passionate about acting; he began auditioning and was cast as a muscleman in *There's Nothing Like A Dame*. Connery continued on his course of self-improvement, studying speech. He began acting in minor TV roles. His first taste of success, came with the telecast of *Requiem for a Heavyweight*, in which his performance was much appreciated. He went from that success to the role of James Bond.

His first Bond film, *Dr No*, was a huge success. Connery went on to play Agent 007 in *Goldfinger, Thunderball, You Only Live Twice, Diamonds Are Forever* and *Never Say Never Again.*

Unwilling to be typecast, Connery starred in other films as well, including *Murder on the Orient Express, A Bridge Too Far* and *The Untouchables,* for which he won the Academy Award for best supporting actor. *Indiana Jones and the Last Crusade* and *The Hunt for Red October* were also major box-office hits. In 1987, he won the best actor award for his role in *The Name of the Rose*. Connery has worked with famous directors Alfred Hitchcock, Brain De Palma and John Huston, to name a few.

In 1990, Connery received the Lifetime Achievement Award (the highest honor of the British Academy of Film and Television Arts, BAFTA). He also received the Cecil B. DeMille Award in 1995, given by the Hollywood Foreign Press Association. His other awards include the *Legion d'Honneur* and *Commandeur des Arts et des Lettres*, which is the highest civilian honor given in France.

Connery was knighted in 2000. He has been a strong advocate for the greater independence of Scotland and has established a charity supporting deprived children in Edinburgh.

Connery is married to French actress Micheline Roquebrune. At 59, he was named the sexiest man alive by *People Magazine*. When asked about it, he is reported to have remarked, "Well, there aren't many sexy dead men, are there."

Ten years later, when he was 69, he was named sexiest man of the century. In 1999, he received the Kennedy Center Honors from U.S. President Bill Clinton. He also received the *Orden de Manuel Amador Guerrero*, presented to him by Mireya Moscoso, president of Panama.

He has entertained audiences the world over for decades, offering major box-office hits. Although Roger Moore, Pierce Brosnon and Timothy Dalton have played James Bond, it was Connery who first captured the imagination of audiences the world over. He's the original cinematic "Bond, James Bond."

Russell Crowe

BIRTH NAME Russell Ira Crowe
BORN April 7, 1964
DROPPED OUT Auckland Grammar School

B ORN IN STRATHMORE Park, Wellington, New Zealand, Russell Crowe was only four years old when his parent moved their family to Australia. His parents used to cater food to film sets and Russell was only six when he started working as an extra to help his family.

When he was eight, Russell had a small role in the series *Spy Force*. The family returned to New Zealand when Russell was 14. There he dropped out of school to help support the family, eventually moving back to Australia when he was 21.

Crowe was drawn towards music and became a rock 'n' roller in his late teens. Because he could not earn enough money to pay his bills by just playing music, he started working as a waiter. He did all sorts of odd jobs for a living, including tending bar and selling insurance. He loved music and acting and worked hard towards this goal. He performed in several stage productions, including *Blood Brothers, Grease* and *The Rocky Horror Show*.

Crowe soon started looking for more challenging roles. In 1990, he acted in *Blood Oath*. He also acted in a comedy, *The Efficiency Expert*. His first major breakthrough though, was in the action flick *Romper Stomper*. This film brought him much acclaim in America. This was followed by a great performance in *The Quick and the Dead*. He performed alongside Denzel Washington in *Virtuosity*, in which he played the role of a man possessed.

Crowe's performance in *LA Confidential* was well received; he described this role as the hardest he had done to that point. He stopped drinking for five months to play the character Bud White. Crowe is an actor who's not scared of the camera. He once said,

"When you're a kid and you get the opportunity to see the technical side of it all, it loses its strangeness. I was exposed to it from such a young age, the camera doesn't scare me."

Crowe's performance in the film *The Insider* got him an Oscar nomination. He won the Academy Award for his role as Maximus, a Roman general who becomes a gladiator, in the hugely successful film *The Gladiator*. On receiving the award, Crowe is reported to have said, "If you grow up in the suburbs of anywhere, a dream like this seems kind of vaguely ludicrous and completely unattainable...this moment is directly connected to those imaginings. And for anybody who's on the downside of advantage and relying purely on courage, it's possible." This was Crowe's way of spreading hope to others.

His dazzling performance in *The Gladiator* also won Crowe the best actor awards from the Broadcast Film Critics Association, San Diego Film Critics and Dallas Forth Worth film Critics Association. In *A Beautiful Mind,* he played a mathematician suffering from schizophrenia who, in trying to overcome the affliction, saves his broken marriage and goes on to win the Nobel Prize. Both Jennifer Connelly, who played the female lead, and Crowe went on to win the Golden Globe and BAFTA awards for their impressive performances in the film.

Crowe had his own rock band, 30 Odd Foot of Grunts, formed in 1992; he was the lead singer and guitarist. The group released three albums, *Gaslight, Bastard of Life or Clarity* and *Other Ways of Speaking,* before disbanding.

Crowe is married to Australian singer and actress Danielle Spencer. The famous New Zealand cricketers Martin Crowe and Jeff Crowe are his cousins. He was once referred to as the "singing cousin of the cricketing Crowes," a description Russell did not like at all.

Tom Cruise

BIRTH NAME Thomas Cruise Mapother IV
BORN July 3, 1962
DROPPED OUT Glen Ridge High School

TOM CRUISE, THE hugely popular movie star was, born in Syracuse, New York. His parents were always on the move and Tom was therefore exposed to life across America at a young age. He attended fifteen different schools by the time he was 14.

His parents divorced when Tom was 12. His mother, Mary Lee, took Tom and his three sisters to Kentucky, where they met with one struggle after another. Tom started delivering newspapers to support the family. When he was in school, he took part in a musical *Guys and Dolls.* Inspired by the applause he got that night, he decided to make acting his career. When his mother remarried and moved the family to New Jersey, Tom dropped out of high school to pursue an acting career in New York.

At 18, Cruise moved to New York. He took up various odd jobs and started working in a restaurant. In the evenings, he attended drama classes. He also started auditioning for TV commercials. He was often turned down, but Cruise was a survivor. He signed up with the Creative Artists Agency to get work in movies.

In 1981, at 19, Cruise got a part in *Endless Love.* His role in *Risky Business* as a Ray Ban–sporting, smart teenager created a sensation. His next movie was Francis Ford Coppola's *The Outsiders.*

Cruise's first major hit was Top Gun, where he played the role of a fighter pilot to perfection, winning him a huge following of fans. He starred in other successful movies, including *The Color of Money, Rain Man* and *Born on the Fourth of July.* Other major hits were soon to follow. *Mission Impossible, Minority Report, Collateral* and *Jerry Maguire.* He also starred opposite Jack Nicholson in *A Few Good Men.* Cruise received Academy Award nominations for his performances in *Born on the Fourth of July* and *Jerry Maguire*. He also received an Oscar nomination for best supporting actor for his role in *Magnolia*.

Cruise was named the top moneymaking star at the box office, in the Quigley Publications annual poll, six times between 1986 and 2001. In 1990, he was chosen as the sexiest man alive by *People Magazine*. In 1995, *Empire Magazine* (U.K.) ranked him one of the sexiest stars in film history; and, in 1997, the same magazine ranked him in the top 100 movie stars of all time. Cruise received the John Huston Award for artists' rights in 1998.

On winning so many awards, Tom has said, "Awards are wonderful. I've been nominated many times and I've won many awards. But my journey is not towards that. If it happens, it will be a blast. If it doesn't, it's still been a blast."

Cruise has contributed to charities that include The Ashley Flint Fund, The Tsunami Relief Fund and The Church of Scientology, as well as to the political campaign of Hillary Rodham Clinton.

Matt Damon

BIRTH NAME Matthew Paige Damon
BORN October 8, 1970
DROPPED OUT Harvard

MATT DAMON WAS born in Cambridge, Massachusetts. In school, he was a straight A student. His mother, a professor of education, helped him with his studies while his father, an investment banker, introduced him to baseball.

Matt's parents separated when he was still very young. He moved with his mother nearer to Harvard. When Matt was ten, he met Ben Affleck, who lived a few blocks down the street. The two enjoyed playing baseball and attended Rindge & Latin School together.

From an early age Damon realized that he wanted to be an actor. He worked hard at it and trained under Gerry Specca, his drama coach at school. He wanted to move to New York for better prospects in acting, but his parents were against the idea. He had some money in a joint account where he and Affleck put their earnings from some television commercials. Damon used the money to move to New York.

Damon got a small role in the film *Mystic Pizza* in 1998. He went on to act in *Rising Son* and *School Ties*. He then bagged a major role in *Geronimo: An American Legend,* a big-budget film that did not do well at the box office. He excelled in his role as a Gulf War veteran in *Courage Under Fire,* earning critical acclaim. This was his first major success. Damon is reported to have dropped 40 pounds for his role in the film.

Later, Damon did gain admission to Harvard, thanks to his excellent academic record. He dropped out just twelve credits short of graduation, to pursue his acting career.

Although Damon had acted in several films by now, he realized the importance of a good screenplay for the success of any film. He started working on this idea. He reworked a script he had written in his Harvard days and asked the famous scriptwriter William Goldman to improvise the dialogue. He sold the script to Miramax and that was how the film *Good Will Hunting* was made. The film went on to win the Academy Award for best screenplay. Damon was nominated for an Oscar for his performance in the film. He and Affleck also received a Golden Globe nomination for the film's screenplay, and Damon got a Golden Globe nomination for best actor in the film.

Damon worked with famous director Steven Spielberg in *Saving Private Ryan*. In 1997, he starred in *Chasing Amy*. He also performed in Francis Ford Coppola's *The Rainmaker*.

After the success of *Good Will Hunting*, Damon and Affleck started Pearl Street Productions, along with friend and associate producer Chris Moore. The company, now known as LivePlanet, promotes good screenplays and funds film projects to help upcoming filmmakers. The first two films made under this project, called Project Greenlight, are *Stolen Summer* and *The Battle of Shaker Heights*.

Damon starred in the film *The Talented Mr Ripley*, again earning a Golden Globe nomination. He learned to play piano for his role in the film. He also worked with director Robert Redford in *The Legend of Bagger Vance* and in *All the Pretty Horses* for director Billy Bob Thornton. After the success of *Ocean's Eleven*, he starred again in *Ocean's Twelve* alongside George Clooney, Brad Pitt and Julia Roberts, among others. His boyish charm, combined with acting skill, has made Matt Damon one the most sought-after stars in Hollywood.

Robert De Niro

BIRTH NAME Robert De Niro Jr.

BORN August 17, 1943

DROPPED OUT High School of Music and Art

ROBERT DE NIRO was born in New York City. His father, Robert De Niro Sr., was a painter, poet and sculptor; and his mother, Virginia Admiral, was also a painter. They divorced when Robert Jr. was two. He lived with his mother, but he also spent time with his father, who took him out to watch movies. He was fascinated by movies and would eenact some of the scenes at home.

De Niro loved acting. When he was 10, he played the role of the cowardly lion in a local production of *The Wizard of Oz*. When he was 17, he enrolled in the High School of Music and Art in New York. He dropped out in his senior year to study with Stella Adler at her conservatory. In 1965, he had a small part in the French film *Three Rooms in Manhattan*. This was followed by Brian DePalma's *Greetings* in 1968 and *Hi, Mom* in 1970. He also appeared in *Bloody Mama, Born to Win, Jennifer on My Mind* and *The Gang That Couldn't Shoot Straight*.

His gained attention in 1973, in *Bang the Drum Slowly*. He played the role of Bruce Pearson, a major league baseball player who suffers from Hodgkin's disease. He went on to win the New York Film Critics Award for his startling performance in this film. That same year, in *Mean Streets*, he began his partnership with Martin Scorsese that would last for decades. He starred in several of Scorcese's films, including *Taxi Driver, New York, New York, Raging Bull, The King of Comedy, Goodfellas, Cape Fear* and *Casino*.

Taxi Driver, in which De Niro played the role of a psychotic cabbie, earned him his first Oscar nomination for best actor. He received the Academy Award for best supporting actor for his portrayal of the young Vito Corleone in the flashback sequence of *The Godfather*

Part II, in 1974. He spent four months learning to speak the Sicilian dialect to play the role of Vito Corleone. His performance as a charismatic movie producer in *The Last Tycoon* was well received, too.

De Niro is an intense actor and a perfectionist. He has played a variety of roles, choosing his parts very carefully. He gained 60 pounds to play Jake La Motta, a middle-aged, brutal, confused boxer in *Raging Bull,* for which he won the Academy Award for best actor. For his role in the musical *New York, New York,* he learned to play the saxophone. In *Angel Heart* (1987) he played the sinister character of Louis Cyphre. In *The Untouchables,* he played Al Capone, the kingpin of crime in Chicago.

De Niro did not shy away from comedy roles either. He acted in *Brazil, Midnight Run, Wag the Dog* and *Analyze This.* He also acted in the comedy *Meet the Parents,* for which he received a Golden Globe nomination. He followed that up with *Meet the Fockers,* which broke box-office records.

Robert De Niro followed his early passion and rose to the top of his profession through commitment and hard work.

Johnny Depp

BIRTH NAME John Christopher Depp II

BORN June 9, 1963

DROPPED OUT Miramar High School

JOHNNY DEPP WAS born in Owensboro, Kentucky. His father, John Christopher Depp Sr., was an engineer; and his mother, Betty Sue, was a waitress. Johnny was very close to his grandfather, who died when Johnny was seven. Soon after, the family moved to Miramar, Florida.

Depp's mother gave him a guitar and he started playing in garage bands at around 13.

Depp's parents divorced. when he was 15. He did not do well in his studies and dropped out of high school, to become a rock singer. He joined a local band, The Kids, the next year. He earned $25 a night playing at clubs. As he was underage, he had to enter these establishments through a back entrance and leave after the first set.

The Kids later changed their name to Six Gun Method and moved to Los Angeles. Depp supported himself with odd jobs, at one point becoming a telemarketer for ballpoint pens. He married make-up artist Lori Anne Allison, who introduced him to Nicolas Cage. Cage urged Depp to get into acting and introduced him to his agent. Depp's debut role was as teenager Glen Lantz in *A Nightmare on Elm Street*. Although the film did well, not many good roles came his way. He faced financial problems that affected on his marriage, which soon ended in divorce.

Depp's wanted to be taken seriously as an actor; he studied at the The Loft, an acting school in Los Angeles. He acted in Oliver Stone's Vietnam drama *Platoon*. That was his last good role for a while. When asked to do a role in *21 Jump Street*, he almost rejected the offer, but agreed to do it after much persuasion. Depp's performance as undercover cop Tom Hanson in the television series gained him loyal fans, but he did not like his newfound status of teen-heartthrob. Looking for a new image, Depp acted in director Tim Burton's *Edward Scissorhands.* He went on to show that he could play serious and quirky roles with ease, in *The Curse of the Black,* a comedy; *Donnie Brasco,* a drama; and *Once Upon a Time in Mexico,* an action thriller.

Depp acted in other Burton films, such as *Ed Wood, Sleepy Hollow, Charlie and the Chocolate Factory* and *Corpse Bride.* More recently, Depp starred in *Pirates of the Caribbean: The Curse of the Black Pearl.* For that film he received an Oscar nomination for his performance as Captain Jack Sparrow. In 2004, he acted in *Secret Window,* based on Stephen King's book. He also costarred with Kate Winslet in *Finding Neverland.*

Depp received a Star on the Hollywood Walk of Fame in 1999.

Johnny Depp has worked hard to perfect his craft and live life on his own terms. He is associated with efforts by the Entertainment Industry Foundation and the National Arts Institute to give children more access to the arts, a cause close to his heart.

ΩΩΩΩΩΩ

Leonardo DiCaprio

BIRTH NAME Leonardo Wilhelm DiCaprio
BORN November 11, 1974
DROPPED OUT John Marshall High School

LEONARDO DICAPRIO, WHO rose to fame with his performance in Titanic, was born in Los Angeles, California. His father, George DiCaprio, was a comic book distributor. His mother, Irmalin Idenbirkin, was a legal secretary who later went on to become her son's manager.

Although his parents divorced when Leonardo was barely a year old, they both remained involved in his upbringing. When Leonardo was still very young, he tap-danced on stage in front of a huge crowd of spectators. That was when his stage fear, if any, disappeared completely. At five, he was on his favorite show, *Romper Room,* almost getting fired for misbehaving on the set. As a child he acted in over 30 televison commercials.

DiCaprio attended the Los Angeles Centre for Enriched Studies, a school for gifted children and the John Marshall High School. He was always more interested in entertaining his classmates with his dancing skills and playing practical jokes and pranks on them than he was in his studies, though, and he eventually dropped out of high school.

DiCaprio was keen on improving his acting skills; he attended acting courses in summer. When he was 17, he found an agent—and refused the agent's suggestion that he change his name.

DiCaprio acted in educational films such as *Mickey's Safety Club* and *How to Deal With a Parent Who Takes Drugs,* as well as televison shows like *Lassie* and *The Outsiders.* His first movie role was as Josh in *Critters 3: You Are What They Eat,* in 1991. His role as Tobias Wolff in *This Boy's Life* won him rave reviews. His performance as Johnny Depp's retarded kid brother in *What's Eating Gilbert Grape* was convincing enough to earn an Oscar nomination and a Golden Globe nomination. He went on to star in a variety of roles—a junkie in *The Quick and the Dead,* a gunslinger in *Batman Forever* and a bisexual poet in *Total Eclipse.*

It was, however, DiCaprio's dazzling performance in James Cameron's *Titanic,* opposite Kate Winslet, in 1997, that catapulted him to fame, winning him a huge fan following. The movie itself got 14 Oscar nominations, and went on to win 11 Academy Awards. In fact he became so famous that it was hard for him to cope.

After *Titanic,* DiCaprio starred in *The Man in the Iron Mask* and Woody Allen's *Celebrity.* His performance in *Catch Me If you Can* won him a Golden Globe nomination. However, it is for his performance in *Titanic* that Leonardo DiCaprio will be remembered for a long time to come.

Jamie Foxx

BIRTH NAME Eric Marlon Bishop

BORN December 13, 1967

DROPPED OUT U.S. International University, San Diego

JAMIE FOXX WAS born in Terrell, Texas. When Jamie was seven months old, his grandparents adopted him, as his teenage mother could not take care of him. He had a disciplined childhood, attending church choir and taking part in Boy Scouts. He also played the piano in churches to earn some money.

His talent as a comedian developed early in life. When he was in the second grade, his teacher used him as a reward, telling the class that Jamie would tell them jokes if they behaved. Jamie was good at sports as well, and was on his high school's football team. In 1989, he moved to Los Angeles and started performing in comedy clubs. He performed at The Improv, The Comedy Store and the Apollo Theater in Harlem. He acted in several comedy shows on television, including the popular show *In Living Color* and his own sitcom *The Jamie Foxx Show*.

In 1992, Foxx got his first movie role, in *Toys*. He later rose to prominence with his performance as a quarterback in Oliver Stone's *Any Given Sunday*. Some of the other films he has acted in are *Booty Call*, *Date from Hell* and *Ali*. In 1994, he performed opposite Tom Cruise in the action flick *Collateral*. He portrayed Ray Charles in the film *Ray*. He gave a stunning performance as Stanley Williams, a death row inmate and Nobel Prize nominee, in *Redemption*. He received three Golden Globe nominations that year—on his 37th birthday—for his performances in those three films and was the first person to be nominated for three Golden Globe awards in the same year. He also won the best actor Oscar for *Ray*.

Foxx has a successful music career, too. He sang the theme song for *Any Given Sunday*. In 1994, he released the album *Peep This*.

He performed live with Alicia Keys and Quincy Jones at the 2005 Grammy Awards and sang "Georgia on My Mind" as a tribute to the late Ray Charles. He also hosted the 2001 MTV Video Music Awards.

Foxx was named one of the 50 most beautiful people by *People Magazine* in 2005. He is only the second male ever to receive two acting Oscar nominations in the same year for two different movies (the first was Al Pacino).

About playing different characters, Foxx once said, "I know people who stay in character, and it's the worst thing in the world. You can't go out. They're still in their character and the character residue is too much. I like to go do it, flip it on like a light switch and then flip it off. Then, when we come back in the next morning I flip it back on. That's what keeps things fresh for me."

In an emotional speech after receiving the Academy Award, Foxx said, "This is going to be the toughest part of this speech. My daughter shares my grandmother's name, Marie. My grandmother's name is Estelle Marie Talley. She's not here tonight. And this is going to be the toughest part. But she was my first acting teacher. She told me to stand up straight. Put your shoulders back. 'Act like you've been somewhere.' And then when I would act the fool, she would beat me. And after she whipped me, she would talk to me why she whipped me. She said I want you to be a southern gentleman. She still talks to me now. Only now, she talks to me in my dreams. And I can't wait to go sleep tonight because we got a lot to talk about. I love you."

Through his ups and downs he will be known as a southern gentleman who beat the odds. He continues to change his character and develop himself as an actor and comedian.

Cuba Gooding Jr.

BIRTH NAME Cuba Gooding Jr.
BORN January 2, 1968
DROPPED OUT High School

CUBA GOODING JR. was born in The Bronx, New York. He's an actor who has climbed up the ladder of success the hard way. His childhood had many ups and downs.

His father, Cuba Gooding Sr., was the lead vocalist of the group The Main Ingredient, of "Everybody Plays the Fool" fame. In 1972, his father moved the family to Los Angeles. He abandoned them two years later. After his parents divorced, Cuba Jr., his brother, mother and sister faced tough times. Life was not the same for them anymore. They went from living in a big house with chauffeurs to being evicted and even living in a car for a brief period. They were also forced onto the welfare rolls for some time. For a boy who had seen the highs of show business the move away from the limelight and the financial hardship that came with it must have been quite a blow. Although Cuba Jr. attended four different schools, he always did well and was elected class president in three of them.

It was at this time, when the family was staying in a motel in Orange County, that Gooding. met Shawn Suttles and Derek Broes. The three of them called themselves the Majestic Vision Break Dancers, and their break dancing moves got them a chance to perform at the end of the 1984 Olympic Games with the famous singer Lionel Richie on stage. Gooding was only sixteen at the time. He enjoyed the attention and soon started taking acting lessons. He also studied Japanese martial arts for three years.

His first role was as a thug in the show *Hill Street Blues*, followed by small roles in other shows like *Jake and the Fatman* and *The Bronx Zoo*. This was followed by a brief role in *Coming to America*. It was however, the lead role in John Singleton's debut movie, *Boys 'N the*

Hood, in 1991 that gave him his major breakthrough. His sensitive portrayal of a young black man growing up in a South Central Los Angles ghetto won him much acclaim.

Gooding went on to win roles in movies like *A Few Good Men, Lightning Jack, Judgment Night* and *Outbreak.* His outstanding performance in *Outbreak* brought him instant recognition. When a last-minute replacement was needed for the role of Rod Tidwell in Cameron Crowe's *Jerry Maguire,* Gooding auditioned for the part. At five-eleven, he was short for the part, but his performance convinced the producers that he was ideal for the role. In the end, the role got him the Academy Award for best supporting actor. He also won a Golden Globe nomination for his acting.

He acted in additional movies, including *As Good as it Gets* and *What Dreams May Come.* He played the role of an ambitious psychiatrist in *Instinct,* receiving good reviews for his acting although the film itself did not do well. He also performed in the film *Chill Factor* and acted opposite Robert de Niro in *Men of Honor.*

In 1997, Gooding was chosen by *People Magazine* as one of the 50 most beautiful people in the world. More recently, he won critical acclaim for his sensitive portrayal of a mentally handicapped man in the film *Radio.* He earned a star on the Hollywood Walk of Fame in the 2002.

He married his high school sweetheart, Sara Kapfer, in 1994. Cuba Gooding Jr. had an uncertain and insecure childhood, but with determination and hard work he gained immortality on the Hollywood Walk of Fame.

Tom Hanks

BIRTH NAME Thomas John Hanks

BORN July 9, 1956

DROPPED OUT California State University

WITH HIS NICE-GUY looks and versatile acting, Tom Hanks has won the hearts of millions of fans, making him a much sought after actor in Hollywood. He has an unending list of hits to his credit, such as *Big, Forest Gump, You've Got Mail, Road to Perdition* and *Cast Away,* to name a few.

Tom Hanks was born in Concord, California. His parents separated when he was young. He spent his childhood moving from place to place with his father, Amos, who was a chef. Tom had to cope with so many changes in his childhood that it prompted him to say, "By the time I turned ten, I had already had three mothers, five grammar schools and ten houses."

Hanks completed Skyline High School in Oakland, California, and went on to California State University, Sacramento, to study theatre. When he did not get a role in a college play, he auditioned for a local theatre; the director of the play invited him to Cleveland. In Cleveland, Hanks first acted in *The Taming of the Shrew,* earning $210 a week. Later, he played Proteus in *Two Gentlemen of Verona* and won the best actor award from the Cleveland Critics Circle.

By age 22 he had already tasted a bit of success. He moved to New York and won a role in the TV sitcom *Bosom Buddies.* It ran two seasons before it was canceled, and Hanks was out auditioning again. He got a role in the movie *Splash,* where he played a nice guy who has an affair with a mermaid. He acted in *The Money Pit,* a slapstick comedy, followed by *Every Time We Say Goodbye,* a film set in Jerusalem. This was his first romantic role in a serious film. His first blockbuster hit was Penny Marshall's *Big.* He played the role of a little boy trapped in a man's body so convincingly that he won the Golden Globe Award, the Los Angeles Film Critics Award and his first Oscar nomination. In 1993, Hanks's sensitive portrayal of an AIDS-afflicted lawyer in *Philadelphia,* won him an Oscar and the Golden Globe Award for best actor. In 1995, he captured the hearts of his fans with his unforgettable performance in *Forest Gump,* winning another Oscar. Hanks is the first actor in fifty years to get two consecutive Academy Awards for best actor.

Hanks has gone on to give memorable performances in the romantic comedy *You've Got Mail,* Steven Spielberg's *Saving Private Ryan* and the space epic *Apollo 13.* His passion for space was dramatized in HBO's *From Earth to the Moon.* The series won 17 Emmy nominations and was also named the year's best miniseries by both the TV Academy and the Hollywood Foreign Press Association.

Tom Hanks is the youngest recipient ever of the American Film Institute's Life Achievement Award. He also was honored with the Distinguished Public Service Award, the U.S. Navy's highest civilian honor, on Veterans Day of 1999, for his work in the movie *Saving Private Ryan.*

Dustin Hoffman

BIRTH NAME Dustin Lee Hoffman
BORN October 8, 1937
DROPPED OUT Santa Monica City College

DUSTIN HOFFMAN WAS born in Los Angeles, California. After graduation from Los Angles High School in 1955, he entered the Los Angeles Conservatory of Music, because he had always dreamed of becoming a concert pianist. He later enrolled at Santa Monica College. He soon dropped out because he was getting poor grades. He took up acting classes for two years at the Pasadena Playhouse, where he met Gene Hackman.

As a young adolescent Hoffman was shy, insecure and self-conscious. A bad bout of acne only added to the problem. His short stature and unconventional looks were not considered ideal for the typical leading man role and he was always being told so. As he himself put it, "I grew up thinking a movie star had to be like Rock Hudson or Tab Hunter, certainly nobody in any way like me."

Wanting to be an actor, Hoffman moved into Gene Hackman's one-bedroom apartment in New York and slept on the kitchen floor. Hoffman took up various odd jobs in order to survive. He worked as a typist, a waiter and a salesman. He took small television roles and stopped acting for a while to take up a teaching job. He once said "I lived below the official American poverty line until I was 31."

The Time Makes Out, 1967, was his first film. It was, however, his convincing performance in *The Graduate,* 1967, that got him his first big break and an Oscar nomination for best actor. His role as a street hustler in *Midnight Cowboy,* 1969, won him another Oscar nomination. He silenced his critics with his versatility as an actor, performing in *Lenny, All the President's Men, Marathon Man* and *Kramer vs. Kramer.* In *Little Big Man,* he played a character who aged from 17 to age 121 (the greatest age span portrayed by a movie actor according to the *Guinness Book of World Records*). He won his first Academy Award, for best actor, for his performance in *Kramer vs. Kramer*. Among his most difficult roles were those in *Tootsie* and *Rain Man*. In *Tootsie*, he played an unsuccessful actor who disguises himself as a woman to become a television star. He was an autistic savant in *Rain Man*, a role for which he won another best actor Oscar. His sensitive and accurate portrayal of a disabled person touched the hearts of many.

Hoffman took time off to study method acting under Lee Strasberg. Hoffman is known for being a perfectionist, so much so that on receiving the Oscar for *Tootsie*, Director Sydney Pollack said, "I'd give it up, if I could have back the nine months of my life I spent with Dustin Hoffman making it." Hoffman is known for endless suggestions, revisions and ideas. While shooting for *Finding Neverland*, 2004, he actually lost the tip of his finger but still continued the day's shooting on morphine. He allegedly kept himself awake for days to appear tired for a scene in *Marathon Man*.

His more recent performances have been in *Midnight Mile*, a romantic comedy; *Confidence*, a crime drama; *Runaway Jury*, alongside his friend Gene Hackman; and *Finding Neverland*, the story of J.M. Barrie's experiences that led to the creation of *Peter Pan*.

Hoffman has his own production company, Punch Productions, which has produced several films in which Hoffman has starred. These include *Tootsie, Hero* and *Wag the Dog*. With his great performances, he has disproved all those who dismissed him as not likely to succeed.

Ashton Kutcher

BIRTH NAME Christopher Ashton Kutcher
BORN February 7, 1978
DROPPED OUT University of Iowa

ASHTON KUTCHER WAS born in Cedar Rapids, Iowa, to Dianne Portwood and Larry Kutcher. He has an older sister, Tausha, and a fraternal twin brother, Michael. Michael was born with a serious heart disease, but survived after a transplant. When Kutcher was thirteen, his parents divorced. When he was fifteen, his mother and stepfather, Mark, moved to Homestead, Iowa.

At school, Kutcher was good at wrestling and football. He was also fond of the stage and took part in plays and musicals. He acted in *The Crying Princess* and *The Golden Goose* while he was still in the seventh grade. In 1997, he joined the University of Iowa to study biochemical engineering, hoping that he could contribute in some way to help people suffering from diseases such as the one that had afflicted his brother. He worked hard during those days to pay for his college tuition; he swept cereal dust from the floor at the General Mills plant in Cedar Rapids, earning twelve dollars an hour. He also washed dishes and donated blood to make some money.

An agent looking for models one day noticed Kutcher at a burger joint. He asked Kutcher to take part in the 1997 Fresh Faces of Iowa modeling contest. Kutcher won the contest and dropped out of college to take up modeling as a career. The prize included a trip to New York City to take part in the 1997 International Model and Talent Association competition. Although he did not win, Kutcher signed up with a reputable agency and went to Milan and Paris, modeling for Versace, Calvin Klein and Tommy Hilfiger. Kutcher, who always loved acting, soon began auditioning for television roles. He signed up for *That 70's Show,* which became a major hit, running for seven years. He rose to fame with the show's success. He also hosted MTV's *Punk'd*. Not wanting to rest on his laurels, he tried his luck on the big screen, too. He acted in the romantic comedy *Down to You*. He also acted in the action film *Reindeer Games*. Kutcher is known to choose his roles with care. More recently, in 2004, he acted in the film *The Butterfly Effect*.

In this film, Kutcher played the role of Evan Treborn, a young man who travels back in time and into his childhood to change the present. Every time he does so, the present goes from bad to worse.

On his role in this film, Kutcher says, "I thought that it was a fantastic metaphor for life, and pretty enlightening. And I appreciated the opportunity to play a character that's blind to the trauma that takes place in his life. The violence that is in the movie I thought was a fantastic metaphor for how blind we are as a society, and as a people, to the things that actually do happen on a day to day basis, and how we kind of just block them out. And whether it be through our media or whatever, we go 'Oh, it's not happening in my world,' so it's not happening."

Other noteworthy films he has starred in are *Texas Rangers, Just Married* and *A Lot Like Love*. He once said, "I will probably never be the best actor in Hollywood, but I hope to be the hardest working."

Brad Pitt

BIRTH NAME William Bradley Pitt

BORN December 18, 1963

DROPPED OUT University of Missouri

BRAD PITT WAS born in Shawnee, Oklahoma. Brad, his sister Julie and his brother Doug grew up in Springfield, Missouri. His father, Bill, worked in a trucking firm and his mother, Jane, was a high school counselor. Brad was greatly influenced by his father's passion for hard work. He once said, "Where I grew up, you deal. You get through it, power through it, straight up the middle. And you don't complain." This never-say-die attitude has helped Pitt reach where he has today.

Pitt went to Kickapoo High School and was good at everything—music; debate; and sports (he was fond of golf, tennis and swimming). At the University of Missouri he studied journalism. Although he had not had any real acting experience, he suddenly decided that he would make acting his career, taking everyone by surprise. Just two credits short of graduating, he moved to California with only a few dollars in his pocket.

Pitt moved into a friend's apartment for a month for free. Later, he shared an apartment with other guys. The apartment was almost empty, with no furniture and no appliances; and all of them had to sleep on the floor. Pitt worked at odd jobs to survive. At one point, he even dressed up as a chicken when he was working for a restaurant chain, El Pollo Loco. He worked as a delivery boy, salesman and assistant. He even drove strippers around in a limousine.

Pitt worked hard at being an actor and took acting lessons from Roy London for six years. He soon won a role in the sitcom *Head of the Class* and also worked in an episode of *Growing Pains*. He played Shalane McCall's boyfriend in Charles in *Dallas*. His first movie role was in *Less than Zero*, followed by Charlie Sheen's *No Man's*

Land and *Cutting Class*. He got a great role in *Dark Side of the Sun*, which was filmed in Yugoslavia; but civil war broke out and the film was lost. Pitt's first big attempt had an unsuccessful end.

He later acted in a TV movie, *Too Young to Die*, with Juliette Lewis, and it was a big success. That was followed by a good role in *Glory Days*, but the show was taken off after six episodes.

Pitt's first claim to fame was his role in Robert Redford's *A River Runs Through It*. After this he started getting great roles. He starred in several popular films, including *True Romance, Interview with the Vampire, Twelve Monkeys, Seven Years in Tibet, Full Frontal, Confessions of a Dangerous Mind, Ocean's Eleven, Ocean's Twelve and Mr. and Mrs. Smith*.

His performance in *Twelve Monkeys*, a brilliant science fiction film, won him the Golden Globe. He also got an Academy Award nomination for best supporting actor in the film. In 1997, *People Magazine* chose him as one of the 50 most beautiful people in the world. In 1995, *Empire Magazine* selected him as one of the 100 sexiest stars in film history. In 1994, *People Magazine* gave him the title Sexiest Man Alive.

Pitt has been generous, donating $100,000 to the Discovery Center, a children's learning museum in his hometown of Springfield, for example.

Brad Pitt is one of the most successful stars in Hollywood. His passion for acting, hard work and dedication have helped him achieve the position he has today.

Sidney Poitier

BIRTH NAME Sidney Poitier

BORN February 2, 1927

DROPPED OUT High School

SIDNEY POITIER WAS born in Miami, Florida. His parents, who were farmers, used to visit Miami regularly to sell tomatoes they grew back home in the Bahamas. Sidney was born in Miami on one such visit.

Poitier grew up on Cat Island and in Nassau, in the Bahamas. He started working full time for a living early in life dropping out of school when he was 13. He lived for a while in Miami with his brother, then moved to New York City, alone, with $3 in his pocket, when he was 16. He lied about his age to get out of the cold and into the army. Less than a year later, he was back in New York, doing odd jobs, including washing ditches. He answered an ad seeking actors and auditioned for the American Negro Theatre. As he knew nothing of acting and could barely read, the experience was humiliating. Undeterred, he went better prepared again six months later and got a role in *Days of Our Youth*. He went on to act in many roles for the theatre in the days to come.

Poitier's first feature film role was in *No Way Out*, in 1950. It was his performance in the movie *The Blackboard Jungle*, in 1955, that gave him his first major breakthrough. He won the BAFTA best actor award for his role in *The Defiant Ones*, in 1958. He went on to win an Oscar for his performance in *Lilies of the Field*, in 1963. Poitier was the first actor of African descent to win the Academy Award. His performance in the film also won him the Golden Globe. Most of his films did well at the box office, including *To Sir with Love* and *Guess Who's Coming to Dinner*, with Katherine Hepburn and Spencer Tracy, and *In the Heat of the Night*, all in 1967.

Poitier has also directed films, including *Let's Do it Again, Up-*

town, Saturday Night and *Stir Crazy*. He did not act in movies for a while, but came back in the late 1980s to star in films such as *Sneakers,* with Robert Redford; *Shoot to Kill* and *Little Nikita*. He also starred alongside Bruce Willis and Richard Gere in *The Jackal*.

Poitier, with dual U.S. and Bahamian citizenship, was knighted by Queen Elizabeth II in 1974. In 1997, he was appointed ambassador to Japan for the Bahamas. He also received a Lifetime Achievement Award from the Academy of Motion Picture Arts and Sciences in 2002.

Poitier is the author of two autobiographies, *This Life* and *The Measure of a Man: A Spiritual Autobiography*. Sidney Poitier had a difficult childhood and struggled during his early years. He has proved that whatever the odds, determination and hard work can certainly take you places.

Arnold Schwarzenegger

BIRTH NAME Arnold Schwarzenegger
BORN July 30, 1947
DROPPED OUT University of Munich

ARNOLD SCHWARZENEGGER IS one of Hollywood's most successful action heroes. With discipline and determination, he has excelled in everything he set out to do. He started his career in bodybuilding and went on to win many prestigious international awards. With his impressive stunts and one-liners, he rose to fame in action flicks like *Conan the Barbarian* and *The Terminator.* He also made a successful transition to politics, becoming the governor of California.

Schwarzenegger was born in Thal, Austria, to Gustav Schwarzenegger and Aurelia Jadrny. He had a strict upbringing, as his father, a police chief, was a tough disciplinarian. Arnold and his brother Meinhard grew up obedient kids. Till he was fourteen, the family did not have a refrigerator, a telephone or even a proper toilet in the house. Schwarzenegger began bodybuilding and weight lifting when he was still a teenager. He always dreamed of having 20-inch biceps and worked hard towards that goal. In 1966, he joined the University of Munich to study marketing.

When he was 18, Schwarzenegger took part in the Mr. Junior Europe Body Building contest and won the title. Later, he went on to win the Mr. Universe title as well. Schwarzenegger holds the record for winning the most major bodybuilding events in history, winning 13 Mr. Junior Western Europe, 7 Mr. Olympics and 5 Mr. Universe titles. It is not surprising, therefore, that the *Guinness Book of World Records* refers to him as "The most perfectly developed man in the history of the world." But his brother and father could not see him succeed. His brother Meinhard died in a car accident. A few years later, his father died of a stroke.

Having achieved all that he wanted in bodybuilding, Schwarzenegger moved to America to act in films. He acted in *Hercules in New York* (1970) and a few other films. But they did not do that well. Arnold financed and published many fitness books and cassettes and made some money, although success in Hollywood continued to elude him. He acted in *Stay Hungry* (1976), *Scavenger Hunt* (1979) and *The Jayne Mansfield Story* (1980). He won the Golden Globe for his performance in *Stay Hungry*, in which he played a bodybuilder alongside Jeff Bridges.

It was *Conan the Barbarian*, in 1982, that catapulted Schwarzenegger to fame. He met with more success in *Conan the Destroyer* (1984) and *Red Sonja* (1985) following this mega hit. At around the same time, James Cameron's science fiction flick *The Terminator* (1984) was also released and Arnold became a superstar of iconic status. *Terminator 2: Judgment Day* (1991) and *Total Recall* (1990) followed, and they were major successes as well. Moving away from this series, he acted in James Cameron's *True Lies* (1994), which was also a major box-office hit. Arnold has performed many of his own stunts in his films because it was hard to find stunt doubles that matched his size. Billy Lucas, Joel Kramer and Peter Kent are his personal stunt doubles and are his close friends as well.

Schwarzenegger once said, "I didn't leave bodybuilding until I felt that I had gone as far as I could go. It will be the same with my film career. When I feel the time is right, I will then consider public service. I feel that the highest honor comes from serving people and your country."

Schwarzenegger works for various social causes and is married to Maria Shriver, a successful television journalist and Kennedy relative.

John Travolta

BIRTH NAME John Joseph Travolta
BORN February 18, 1954
DROPPED OUT High School

JOHN TRAVOLTA WAS born in Englewood, New Jersey. His father, Salvatore, was in the tire business. His mother, Helen, was a high school drama teacher. She had performed in a radio vocal group, The Sunshine Sisters, and had acted and directed before starting her teaching career. John was the youngest of six children, with two brothers and three sisters. The whole family loved music and theatre. John's father encouraged them by providing a small theatre in the basement.

As a young boy, Travolta loved the stage. He was a great fan of the Beatles. He learned to play the guitar and also won a dance competition when he was still very young. When he was 12, he enrolled in drama school in New York. He was nicknamed Bone because he was very thin. Gene Kelly's brother Fred taught him tap dancing.

When he was 16, Travolta dropped out of high school and moved to Manhattan to become an actor. He worked as a cashier, ticket collector and luggage handler. He acted off-Broadway to gain experience. On television, he acted in a U.S. Army commercial and then got his big break with the show *Welcome Back Kotter*. In 1976, he starred in the TV tearjerker *The Boy in the Plastic Bubble* and became a rage among teenagers.

Travolta moved on to movies. He danced his way to fame in *Saturday Night Fever*, for which he received an Oscar nomination. The 1970s was the disco era and Travolta became an icon. He again sang his way to stardom in the musical *Grease*. He also released several albums, including *Travolta Fever*, for which he won a Billboard Award for best male vocalist.

In the 1980s, Travolta acted in *Two of a Kind* and *Staying Alive*, neither of which did well. There were other flops as well and there was a brief lull in his career; but in 1994, Travolta came back with a vengeance in Quentin Tarantino's *Pulp Fiction*, opposite Uma Thurman, receiving another Oscar nominations for that role. He went on to star in hits like *Get Shorty, The Thin Red Line, A Civil Action* and *The General's Daughter.* He won the Golden Globe for his role in *Get Shorty.*

Meanwhile, Travolta, who believes in Scientology starred in *Battlefield Earth,* based on L. Ron Hubbard's Scientology-based science fiction novel. The movie, which cost upwards of $70 million, did not do well at the box office initially. Instead of wallowing in self-pity, Travolta talked about his involvement in the film and how it was made in the first place. The movie went on to become a cult hit. Travolta's more recent movies are *A Love Song for Bobby Long, The Punisher, Ladder 49* and *Be Cool.*

Travolta owns five airplanes, including a Boeing 707, and loves to fly. He is a skilled pilot and his house in Florida has a runway and taxiway that leads to his doorstep.

John Travolta has had his share of ups and downs in his career, but he has always come back and proved that he's a true Hollywood star.

Bruce Willis

BIRTH NAME Walter Bruce Willison
BORN March 19, 1955
DROPPED OUT Montclair State College

BRUCE WILLIS, THE famous Hollywood actor with die-hard fans, earned his place among the superstars with dedication and hard work. He was drawn towards theatre and acting at an early age. His childhood was not privileged either with wealth or with Hollywood connections. Yet he rose to stardom, becoming one of Hollywood's great action heroes.

Bruce Willis was born on a U.S. military base in Idar-Oberstein, Germany. His family moved to New Jersey when he was barely two. His father was a mechanic. At an early age Bruce or Bruno as he was nicknamed, overcame a speech impediment through acting and rehearsal. He moved to New York to study acting in Montclair State College but dropped out because he got bored.

To make a living as he worked his way into the film industry, Willis took up odd jobs as a bartender and waiter. He made his theatre debut in *Heaven and Earth*, followed by a role in television for *Miami Vice*. Although his film debut was as an extra in the film *The First Deadly Sin*, with Frank Sinatra, his first big success came when he co-starred opposite Cybill Shepherd in the sitcom *Moonlighting*. He won an Emmy and also the Golden Globe Award for his performance in *Moonlighting*.

Willis starred in blockbusters like *Die Hard*, *Pulp Fiction* and M. Night Shyamalan's *Unbreakable*. He also starred in movies like *The Whole Nine Yards*, *Ocean's Twelve* and *Hostage*. His role as detective John McClane in the action flick *Die Hard* brought him instant fame. After *Die Hard*, came *Die Hard 2* and *Die Hard with a Vengeance*.

Another movie that proved to be a huge hit was *The Sixth Sense*, which grossed over six hundred million dollars and was nominated for six Academy Awards. Willis played the role of child psychiatrist Dr. Malcolm Crowe in the movie, for which he won the Best Actor prize in the People's Choice Awards. *Twelve Monkeys, Fifth Element* and *Armageddon* are other box-office hits he starred in.

As an actor, Willis has been versatile playing a variety of roles. He played the role of an abusive husband in *Mortal Thoughts*, opposite Demi Moore, and as a gangster in Billy Bathgate. He has also starred in films like *Death Becomes Her, Color of Night* and *Nobody to Fool*. Willis tried to hone his skills behind the camera as well, as producer of features like *The Crocodile Hunter: Collision Course* and *Hostage*.

The superstar's interest in theatre inspired him to cofound a non-profit theatre group called *A Company of Fools*. He also has a passion for music, the result of which is an album, *Bruce Willis: The Return of Bruno*, for Motown Records, which went platinum. The actor has his own rock band, The Accelerators; and his 1987 cover of "Respect Yourself" was on the top ten list. Known for being outspoken, the actor was vocal about his support for the war in Iraq.

His marriage with actress Demi Moore lasted thirteen years and they have three children. When asked how he feels about being a multimillionaire, Willis's response was, "I'm staggered by that question. I always have to remind myself that I am. I'm much more proud of being a father than being an actor." He has also been a special ambassador of his birthplace Idar-Oberstein, Germany.

With great performance in action films, comedies and even romantic movies, Willis has proved to be a versatile star.

$ **Millionaire Dropouts Trivia** $

America's richest high school dropout, J.R. Simplot, is worth $4.7 billion.

Actresses

Actresses

Actresses

Actresses

Actresses

Actresses

Actresses

Actresses

Actresses

Lucille Ball

BIRTH NAME Lucille Désirée Ball
BORN August 6, 1911
DIED April 26, 1989
DROPPED OUT John Murray Anderson
School for the Dramatic Arts

LUCILLE BALL, ONE of the best-known and most loved stars in the history of American television, was born in Jamestown, New York, in 1911. Her father, Henry Durrell Ball, died in 1915 of typhoid fever; and her mother, Desiree Evelyn Hunt, along with her grandparents, raised her. She joined the John Murray Anderson School for the Dramatic Arts; but, being a shy girl, she was easily surpassed by another student, Bette Davis. She left a few weeks later, on being told by the drama coach that she "had no future at all as a performer."

Ball was successful as a model in the 1930s, working for designer Hattie Carnegie and as a Chesterfield Cigarette Girl. She got a part as a Goldwyn Girl in the musical *Roman Scandals*. Ball moved to Los Angeles at age 22 to pursue her movie career. She appeared in many small roles but was never considered successful and often referred to as a B-movie queen. Some of the movies she did in this period were *Stage Door, Room Service* and *Sorrowful Jones*.

Ball met Desi Arnaz in 1940, on the set of *Too Many Girls*, a film version of the Rodgers and Hart stage production. Arnaz was a bandleader from Cuba. There was an immediate attraction between them, and they eloped the same year. The marriage was not always a happy one, as Arnaz was a philanderer and drank to excess, causing Ball constant grief. She filed for divorce in 1944, after learning of her husband's infidelity, but got back together with him soon after.

With her tireless spirit, Ball decided to try her luck with radio programs. After a number of nonstarters, she finally developed her own style in 1948, at age 37, on a program for CBS called *My Favorite Husband*. The show was a success; and, when she was asked by CBS to develop it into a television program, she insisted on working with Arnaz, in an effort to save her failing marriage. The show was named *I Love Lucy* and became a hit as soon as it aired. Lucille Ball and Desi Arnaz became millionaires. They bought the studio and renamed it Desilu.

After several miscarriages, Ball's first child, Lucie, was born in 1951. Her second child, Desiderio, was born in 1953. As neither parent was willing to take a break, they intended to write the pregnancy into the script. This caused a great controversy with the network, as they refused to let a pregnant woman be shown on television or even to allow the word pregnant to be said on air. In the end, the network agreed to Ball appearing on television but the word *pregnant* could still not be used. Instead she was "expecting."

I Love Lucy ended in 1957, when it was still at its peak. Desilu had produced a few movies and become quite a large company by the late 1950s. The couple's success on the business front was not able to preserve the marriage, and they divorced in 1960. It was the end of television's first family although they remained friends till Arnaz's death in 1986.

In 1961, Ball married comedian Gary Morton. She bought out Arnaz's share of the studio and remained its head but was not actively involved in running it. In the 1960s and 1970s, she produced several television projects and starred in *Yours, Mine and Ours* and *Mame*; the Broadway musical *Wildcat*; and two sitcoms with Gale Gordon, *The Lucy Show* and *Here's Lucy*. Her last show in 1986, called *Life with Lucy* was a decisive flop.

In her lifetime, Lucille Ball received many honors and awards. She won Emmys in 1953, 1956, 1967 and 1968. She was inducted in the Hollywood Walk of Fame, with two stars, one each for movies and television. She died in 1986, of an aneurysm, in Los Angeles. In her memory, the U.S. Postal Service issued a stamp with her image and released it on her birthday, August 6, 2001.

Drew Barrymore

BIRTH NAME Drew Blythe Barrymore
BORN February 22, 1975
DROPPED OUT High School

DREW BLYTHE BARRYMORE was born in Culver City, California, into a family with a long history in acting and theatre. Her father, John Drew Barrymore, was an actor, as is her half-brother John Blyth. Her grandfather was the silent movie legend John Barrymore, and her great aunt was the famous Ethel Barrymore. Her mother, Ildiko Jad Barrymore, usually known as Jaid, is a Hungarian actress.

Drew was a wild child, often in the headlines for excessive partying, drug addiction and attempted suicide. Starting her career in front of the camera before she was a year old, for a dog food commercial, Drew moved steadily to movies, playing the role of a boy in *Suddenly Love* when she was three years old. A year later, she played the part of Margaret Jessup in *Altered States*. Drew's godfather, Steven Spielberg, cast her as Gertie in *E.T. the Extra-Terrestrial* when she was seven, making her a child star.

By the time she was nine, Drew had begun having serious problems with drinking and drugs. She began smoking marijuana when she was 10 and doing cocaine when she was 12. In her autobiography *Little Girl Lost*, written in 1990, Barrymore describes her turbulent childhood and traumatic adolescence and the problems she faced on being successful early in life. Dropping out of school, she acted in films that included *Cat's Eye, See You in the Morning, Far from Home* and *Motorama*. She entered rehab to get cleaned up and returned to movies with a new commitment and respect for her profession. She acted in *Poison Ivy, Guncrazy, Wayne's World 2, The Amy Fisher Story, Bad Girls, Boys on the Side, Batman Forever* and *Scream*.

Since 1996, Barrymore has acted in more romantic comedies, such as *Everybody Says I Love You, Wishful Thinking, The Wedding*

Singer, Ever After: A Cinderella Story and *Home Fries.* Some of her recent movies include *50 First Dates, Duplex, Never Been Kissed,* both *Charlie's Angels* movies and *Fever Pitch.*

Barrymore established a production company in 1998, Flower Films, which produced the blockbusters *Charlie's Angels* and *Never Been Kissed.* The company also did some offbeat films, *Riding in Cars with Boys, Freddy Got Fingered* and *Confessions of a Dangerous Mind,* to counterbalance her sweet romances.

In 2004, Barrymore received a Hollywood Walk of Fame star.

Barrymore was married for six weeks to Jeremy Thomas, a Los Angeles bar owner. In 2001, she married Tom Green, her *Charlie's Angels* costar; but the couple were divorced in October 2002.

After a traumatic childhood and turbulent adolescence, Barrymore is leaving her wild days behind and taking on a womanly persona. She believes in making movies that entertain people rather than only stretching her skills as an actress. An optimist, she believes in happy endings and movies that uplift and empower an individual and brighten the spirit.

At the young age of 30, Drew Barrymore has lived and experienced more success and failures them most people do in a lifetime. She has proven that with enough passion and time anyone can turn their life around to be inspiring and powerful.

Courteney Cox

BIRTH NAME Courteney Bass Cox

BORN June 15, 1964

DROPPED OUT Mount Vernon College

COURTENEY BASS COX was born in Birmingham, Alabama, to an affluent Southern family. She was the youngest of four children, with one brother, Richard, and two sisters, Virginia and Dottie. She was named after her mother, Courteney, but mostly called by her nickname, CeCe. As a child, she lived in Mountain Brook, Alabama, an elite town.

Her father, Richard L Cox, was a businessman who indulged his youngest daughter. When her parents divorced in 1974, Courteney was shattered. Her father moved to Florida and she lived with her mother and new stepfather, Hunter Copeland. She was a cheerleader, tennis player and swimmer in high school.

Her first modeling job came in her final year of high school, for the store Parisian. After graduation, she enrolled in Mount Vernon College to study architecture and interior design but dropped out after the first year, when she was signed by Ford Modeling Agency, to pursue her modeling career. Some of her initial covers were for teen magazines such as *Tiger Beat* and *Little Miss*. Her initial commercials were for Maybelline, Noxzema and Tampax, in which she was the first person to say the word *period* on TV.

Her dream was to be an actress; so she started attending acting classes. Her first part on TV was in 1984, on the soap opera *As the World Turns*. She was selected for Bruce Springsteen's *Dancing in the Dark* video, where he pulled her up onto the stage to dance with him. The resulting publicity led to a job on TV hosting *This Week's Music*. Cox also worked at F.B.I. (Frontier Booking International), a concert-booking agency.

She moved to Los Angeles in 1985 and starred in the movie *Misfits of Science* with Dean Paul Martin. The movie was a flop but, in

1987, she landed a role in the successful show *Family Ties,* as Michael J Fox's bright and perky girlfriend. When the show ended in 1989, she tried her luck at movies but had a disappointing run in her first few movies.

True Hollywood success came in 1994 with *Ace Ventura: Pet Detective* and especially her role as Monica Geller on the hit TV show *Friends.* Cox was originally called to audition for the role of Rachel, but convinced the show's producers to instead give her Monica's role. She was the most famous of the six friends and soon shot to stardom. She was nominated for an American Comedy Award.

Over the years, Cox has received numerous accolades for her beauty and style. She appeared on the cover of *People Magazine* and was included in their list of 50 most beautiful people in 1995. In 2002, *Stuff Magazine* voted her the 18th sexiest woman in the world.

In 1996, Cox starred in the slasher comedy *Scream.* Made by Wes Craven, the movie was an unqualified success and Cox won critical acclaim for her portrayal of a wickedly bitchy TV reporter, Gale Weathers. The movie grossed over $100 million and led to the making of two more movies in the *Scream* trilogy, in which she played the same character.

Cox and David Arquette met and fell in love during the making of Scream in 1996. (He played her love interest in the film as well.) They were engaged in 1998 and married 12 June 1999 at Grace Cathedral in San Francisco. The couple has one child; a daughter named Coco Riley Arquette, born 13 June 2004 in Los Angeles.

Currently, Cox is focusing on her passion for interior design. In June 2004, the couple launched a production company called Coquette. The couple are the executive producers on the show *Mix it Up,* a decorating show where the styles of two individuals clash, much as they do in real life.

Cameron Diaz

BIRTH NAME Cameron Michelle Diaz
BORN August 30, 1972
DROPPED OUT Long Beach Polytechnic High School

CAMERON DIAZ WAS born in San Diego, California. Her father, Emilio Diaz, was an oil company foreman of Cuban-American descent and her mother, Billie, was a businesswoman of English-German-Native American ancestry. Cameron has one sister, Chimene. As a child, Cameron was an adventurous tomboy and strongly independent.

Diaz has always been noticed for her archetypical Californian good looks. When she was sixteen, she met a photographer at a party who helped her get a contract with Elite Modeling Agency. Dropping out of high school, she spent the next five years traveling the world for her modeling assignments. In 1994, she auditioned for a minor role in *The Mask* but was astonished to actually find herself cast as Jim Carrey's love interest in the film.

Being fiercely independent and certain of the direction she wanted her career to take, Diaz played low-profile characters in independent art films for the next few years. Her performances in movies like *The Last Supper, Feeling Minnesota* and *She's the One* were commended. In 1997, she acted in *My Best Friend's Wedding* with Julia Roberts and managed to hold her own. The film was a huge success and brought Diaz out into mainstream Hollywood. It was her next movie, *There's Something About Mary*, that catapulted her to superstardom.

Cameron always believed in taking risks. She returned to independent films in 1999, in *Being John Malkovich*, playing the role of an unkempt, dowdy woman so well that she was transformed and barely recognizable as the glamorous Cameron Diaz. In the same year, she worked in Oliver Stone's *Any Given Sunday*, receiving praise for the depth and range of her performance. In 2000, she landed a role in the highly coveted movie *Charlie's Angels,* co-starring with Drew Barrymore and Lucy Liu. The movie was a huge commercial success and led to the making of a sequel in 2003.

Always mixing it up to keep it interesting, Diaz did projects like, *Things You Can Tell Just by Looking at Her* in 2000, *Vanilla Sky* and *The Invisible Circus* in 2001, *The Sweetest Thing, Slackers* and *Gangs of New York* in 2002. she was also part of *Shrek* in 2001, the most successful animated film to date, and its sequel, *Shrek 2* in 2004.

Diaz is both exuberant and passionate in her beliefs. She believes in leading a life of one's own making by being forthright and independent. She stood her ground, fighting and winning a lawsuit against photographer John Rutter for trying to blackmail her with photographs he had taken in 1992. Growing up with a lot of boys, she has always been active in sports, playing hard enough that she has frequently broken bones, the last being her nose while surfing on her birthday in 2003.

Diaz has always been known for her sexy, sassy image. In 1995, Australia's *Empire Magazine* included her in their list of 100 sexiest stars at number 13 and again at number 11 in 2002. *People Magazine* selected her in their list of 50 most beautiful people in 1998 and again in 2002. Believing in herself and going all out to achieve her goals, Diaz became the second actress in Hollywood, after Julia Roberts, to earn $20 million for a movie contract. That movie was *Charlie's Angles: Full Throttle* in 2003.

Angelina Jolie

BIRTH NAME Angelina Jolie Voight

BORN June 4, 1975

DROPPED OUT New York University Film School

ANGELINA JOLIE WAS born on June 4, 1975 in Los Angeles. She is the daughter of Jon Voight and Marcheline Bertrand. Her father was already a successful star by the time she was born, acting in movies that include *Midnight Cowboy* and *Deliverance*. Her mother was a model of French and Iroquois descent. After her parents divorced, she moved to New York with her mother and her brother James.

As a child, Angelina wanted to be a funeral director, but she developed an interest in film when her mother started taking her to see movies. They moved to Los Angeles when she was 11; and she joined The Lee Strasberg Theatre Institute, training for two years and acting in several plays. She was a misfit in high school, tall and thin, with glasses and braces. These years affected her psyche deeply and taught her to survive and to live life on her own terms.

After some modeling assignments in Los Angeles, New York and London, Jolie starred in *Cyborg 2*, the role that first got her noticed, in 1993. She then acted in *Hackers* with Johnny Lee Miller. They had an instant attraction and soon married. The publicity surrounding *Hackers* and her marriage led to more offers, and she starred in *Playing God, Mojave Moon, Foxfire* and *True Women*.

She played the part of the wife of the segregationist governor of Alabama in *George Wallace*. In her next TV movie, *Gia*, she played the role of Gia Carangi, a lesbian supermodel in the 1970s who lived a dangerous life of sex and drugs and died of AIDS. For each of these films, Jolie won both a Golden Globe and Emmy.

The emotional roller coaster life that Jolie lived was too much for Miller; they divorced in 1999. She moved to New York and enrolled in the Film School at New York University, although she did not graduate. Her next movie was *Pushing Tin,* a comedy drama with Billy Bob Thornton and John Cusack. During the making of the film, Jolie fell in love with and married Thornton, 15 years her senior.

With each role, she was slowly but surely becoming part of mainstream Hollywood. In *Girl, Interrupted,* she played the role of a depressed young woman. Although her co-star, Winona Ryder, was the more popular star, Jolie stole the show and won an Oscar. This was her turning point, from being a weird, offbeat actress to a Hollywood superstar. She acted in big-budget movies like *The Bone Collector, Gone in 60 Seconds, Original Sin* and *Tomb Raider. Tomb Raider* was physically demanding, and she worked hard to do the stunts herself.

Jolie's marriage to Thornton could not survive their divergent interests and they separated in 2002, formally divorcing in 2003. Jolie acted in *Life or Something Like It, Alexander, Sky Captain* and *Tomb Raider: The Cradle of Life.* None was a great hit, but these films kept her in the top tier of Hollywood actresses.

In *Beyond Borders,* she played a role remarkably similar to her own life. In 2004, she acted in *Taking Lives* and was the voice of a fish named Lola in *Shark Tale.* In 2005, spy comedy *Mr. and Mrs. Smith,* co-starring Brad Pitt, opened successfully. The movie, however, was surrounded by the scandalous breakup of Brad Pitt's marriage to Jennifer Aniston and Jolie's involvement in that breakup.

Jolie has two adopted children, Maddox, whom she adopted in 2001 from Cambodia, and Zahara, whom she adopted in 2005 from Ethiopia. The United Nations made her a Good Will Ambassador and she frequently travels to third world countries to raise awareness on health and living conditions. In August 2005, Cambodia's King Norodom Sihanouk awarded her an honorary Cambodian citizenship for her charity and conservation work.

Nicole Kidman

BIRTH NAME Nicole Mary Kidman
BORN June 20, 1967
DROPPED OUT North Sydney Girls High School

NICOLE KIDMAN WAS born in Honolulu, Hawaii, in 1967, to Australian parents; she has dual citizenship in Australia and the United States. Her family lived in Washington, D.C., until Nicole was three and then returned to Australia, where she spent the rest of her childhood. Her father, Dr. Anthony David Kidman, was a cancer research specialist and her mother, Janelle Ann, was a nursing instructor. She has a younger sister, Antonia, an entertainment reporter.

Growing up in Longueville, a suburb of Sydney, Nicole displayed an interest in the performing arts from a young age. She took dance, drama and mime classes, performing at the Philip Street Theatre in Sydney when she was a teenager. Nicole was 15 when she made her film debut, in *Bush Christmas*. After its success, she joined The Disney Channel's *Five Mile Creek*. She decided to drop out of high school, when she realized her talent and looks would take her further. Around this time, her mother was also diagnosed with breast cancer and Nicole focused on family responsibilities.

Some of Kidman's early movies were *BMX Bandits* and *Archer's Adventure*. She also appeared in TV miniseries, including *Vietnam*, 1986; *Emerald City*, 1988; and *Bangkok Hilton*, 1989; but did not gain international attention until she starred in *Dead Calm*, with Sam Neill, in 1989.

Her first big hit was *Days of Thunder*, with Tom Cruise, which led to a whirlwind romance. They were married in 1990 in Telluride, Colorado. The couple adopted two children, Isabella, born in 1992, and Connor, born in 1995, and divided their time between houses in California, Colorado, New York and Australia. In 2001, they divorced.

In the 1990s, Kidman starred in *Far and Away*, with Cruise; *Batman Forever*, with Val Kilmer; *Billy Bathgate*, with Dustin Hoffman; *My Life*, with Michael Keaton; *Practical Magic*, with Sandra Bullock; and *Malice*. All were big-budget movies, but only in Gus Van Sant's *To Die For* was she commended for her performance. In 1999, Kidman acted with husband Tom Cruise in Stanley Kubrick's last movie, *Eyes Wide Shut*, but the movie got mixed reviews.

Although, her first major award was a Golden Globe, in 1996, for *To Die For*, Kidman's career hit an upswing only after her divorce from Cruise. Since then she has won two other Golden Globes, one for *Moulin Rouge*, in 2002, and one for her sensitive portrayal of Virginia Woolf in *The Hours*, in 2003. The same year, she also won a BAFTA and an Oscar for *The Hours*. She was the first Australian actress to receive the Oscar for best actress. She was inducted in the Hollywood Walk of Fame in 2003.

Kidman's willowy beauty has won her many accolades. She is frequently on the best-dressed list and was named as one of the *People Magazine* 50 most beautiful people, for most wanted skin, in 2004. She is reputed to be the richest Australian women under the age of 40 and was listed as the 45th most powerful celebrity on the 2005 Forbes "Celebrity 100" list.

Kidman has received good reviews for her performances in movies including *Portrait of a Lady, Dogville, Birth, Cold Mountain, The Stepford Wives* and *The Peacemaker*. Some of her recent films are *Bewitched* and *The Interpreter*, both released in 2005.

Since 1994, Kidman has been a goodwill ambassador for UNICEF Australia. She has been raising awareness to improve the lives of disadvantaged children around the world, especially in Australia. The UN named her as a citizen of the world in recognition of her humanitarian work, in 2004.

Hilary Swank

BIRTH NAME Hilary Ann Swank
BORN July 30, 1974
DROPPED OUT South Pasadena High School

HILARY SWANK WAS born in Bellingham, Washington, in 1974. She was an athletic child, participating and excelling in gymnastics and swimming. She took part in the Junior Olympics and State Championships, ranking fifth in Washington State for gymnastics. Her first acting role was Mowgli in *The Jungle Book*, in a local stage production, when she was nine.

Hilary's parents divorced when she was 15. A year later she moved with her mother to Los Angeles to pursue an acting career. They had financial problems in Los Angeles, to the extent of living in a car for some time until Hilary got some roles. She dropped out of high school when she was 16 to focus on acting.

Swank appeared in a number of shows on television, including *Evening Shade, Growing Pains, Camp Wilder and Harry* and *the Hendersons*. She began to be noticed after appearing in *Buffy the Vampire Slayer*, in 1992, and *Cries Unheard: The Donna Yaklich Story*, in 1994. These roles led to her landing the title role in *The Next Karate Kid*, in 1994. The movie did average business but led to more offers for Swank.

The late 1990s saw her doing more TV movies, including *Terror in the Family*, 1996, *Leaving LA*, 1997 and *The Sleepwalker Killing*, also in 1997. She was featured in *Beverly Hills 90210* for less than one season but still managed to create a lasting impression.

In 1999, she acted in *Boys Don't Cry*, where she played the role of Brandon Teena. The movie was a true story based on a girl in Lincoln, Nebraska, who pretended to be a boy as a defense strategy after being molested. Swank received critical acclaim and went on to win an Oscar and a Golden Globe for her riveting performance.

She was catapulted to instant stardom with *Boys Don't Cry* and acted in numerous movies, including *The Gift*, 2000, *The Affair of the Necklace*, 2001, *Insomnia*, 2002, *The Core* and *11:14*, both in 2003. In 2004, she acted in the HBO movie *Iron Jawed Angels* with Anjelica Huston and Frances O'Connor. She also narrated the documentary *Reel Models: The First Women of Film*, with Barbara Streisand.

In 2005, Swank won her second Oscar, for *Million Dollar Baby*. The movie was directed by Clint Eastwood and showcased her talent as a driven, no-nonsense performer. To play the part realistically, she diligently trained for over five months and changed her eating habits to put on 15 pounds of muscle. Her only other movie in 2004 was *Red Dust*, directed by Tom Hooper.

Swank met Chad Lowe in 1992 and five years later, on October 2, 1997, they got married. They live in Greenwich Village in New York City. She retains her outdoors interests, going skydiving, river rafting and skiing often.

Despite her success, Hilary Swank remains a grounded and humble person. She credits her screen role as Brandon, in *Boys Don't Cry*, as an inspiration to live her life to its fullest and to not be tied down by others' expectations. She famously remarked on her success when she won her Oscar for *Million Dollar Baby* in 2005, saying: "I don't know what I did in this life to deserve this. I'm just a girl from a trailer park who had a dream."

Uma Thurman

BIRTH NAME Uma Karuna Thurman
BORN April 29, 1970
DROPPED OUT Northfield Mount Hermon School

UMA THURMAN WAS born in Boston, Massachusetts, in 1970. Her father, Robert Thurman, is a professor of Indo-Tibetan Buddhist studies at Columbia University. Her mother, Nena Holmquist, is a former model of Swedish and German descent. Uma was brought up with Buddhist traditions, although she is not overly religious as an adult. She is named after the Hindu goddess of light and beauty. Uma's three brothers, Ganden, Dechen and Mipam are also named for figures in Buddhist mythology. The environment at home was unorthodox: the Dalai Lama occasionally stayed with them on his visits to the U.S..

Thurman was a total misfit in school—tall, skinny and gawky. As the family moved often, she was usually the new student in class, making it even harder to fit in and make friends. She found refuge only on the stage and when acting. When she was 15, she left her boarding school, Northfield Mount Hermon, to go to New York to act professionally.

After a year of modeling and washing dishes to pay the rent, Thurman got a role in *Kiss Daddy Goodnight* in 1987. The movie was a flop but Thurman received good notices. She did a lighthearted romantic comedy, *Johnny Be Good*, next. In 1988, she starred in *The Adventures of Baron Munchausen* and *Dangerous Liaisons*. Thurman was suddenly transformed into a sex symbol. She began to receive offers of major parts.

Making a conscious decision to be selective in her roles, she appeared in *Henry & June* and *Where the Heart Is*, both in 1990. Other movies in this period were *Final Analysis*, in 1992, *Jennifer 8*, in 1992, *Mad Dog and Glory*, in 1993, and *Even Cowgirls Get the Blues*, in

1994. Her breakthrough film was Quentin Tarantino's *Pulp Fiction,* in 1994, for which she received an Oscar nomination for best supporting actress. Her role as Mia Wallace was electric; and the movie was wildly successful, taking Thurman to a cult status.

The late 1990s saw her in *The Truth about Cats & Dogs* and *Beautiful Girls,* which were both reasonably successful, and independent films like *A Month By the Lake,* in 1995. In 1997, on the set of *Gattaca,* she met Ethan Hawke, whom she later married. After acting in two major movies, *Batman and Robin,* in 1997, and *The Avengers,* in 1998, she reunited with Quentin Tarantino for *Kill Bill: Vol. 1* in 2003 and *Kill Bill: Vol. 2* in 2004. Thurman deliberately chooses to do small-budget movies. She appeared in *Sweet and Lowdown,* with Woody Allen and Sean Penn, *Tape,* with Ethan Hawke, and *Hysterical Blindness,* a TV movie directed by Mira Nair.

Thurman married Gary Oldman in 1990, when she was 20; but they divorced after two years. She married Ethan Hawke in 1998. They have two children, Maya, born in 1998, and Roan, born in 2002. The couple separated in 2003 and formally divorced in 2004.

In 2005, Uma acted with John Travolta in *Be Cool,* the sequel to the quirky comedy *Get Shorty,* and also had a part in *The Producers: The Movie Musical.*

Naomi Watts

BIRTH NAME Naomi Watts

BORN September 28, 1968

DROPPED OUT High School

NAOMI WATTS WAS born in Shoreham, England, and spent her childhood in England. Her father, Peter Watts, was a sound engineer for Pink Floyd until 1974; and her mother, Myfanwy "Miv" Watts, was an interior designer and amateur actress of Welsh heritage. Naomi's parents got divorced in 1972 and she lived in Wales, with her grandparents, her mother and brother. Naomi's father died when she was 9. Her brother, Ben Watts, is a fashion photographer.

The family moved to Australia when Naomi was 14. She soon joined acting classes and dropped out of high school. Her first assignment was *For Love Alone* in 1986. After a lull of almost five years, she worked with Nicole Kidman and Thandie Newton in *Flirting*. Watts had met Kidman years earlier, when they both auditioned for the same bikini commercial (they remain good friends).

Over the next ten years, Watts struggled with one flop after another—*Matinee, Tank Girl, Persons Unknown, Brides of Christ, Wide Sargasso Sea, Gross Misconduct* and *Children of the Corn IV: The Gathering.* Her luck changed when she acted in David Lynch's *Mulholland Drive* in 2001. Her performance won praise and, finally, at 34, she was becoming famous. She got the lead role in the remake of *The Ring* in 2002, her biggest success to date.

In 2003, Watts acted in *21 Grams*, a movie she accepted without even reading the script, and was nominated for the Academy Award for best actress. The same year, she acted in *Le Divorce* with Kate Hudson.

Watts did her first comedy, *I Heart Huckabees*, in 2004, as a contrast to the intense roles she usually takes. In 2005, she acted in the remake of *King Kong*, for which she moved to New Zealand for the five-month shoot. Also in 2005, she acted in *The Ring 2*, which had a hugely successful opening weekend and assured her place as a bona fide star and box office draw.

The buzz surrounding Watts led to *Ellie Parker,* an independent film she produced and acted in, in 2001, being featured at the Sundance Film Festival and re-released in December 2005.

The year 2002, was when the world sat up and took notice of Watts's delicate beauty. *People Magazine* included her in their list of 50 most beautiful people. She was voted the 14th sexiest female movie star in September 2002 and appeared on the cover of Australia's *Empire Magazine. Forbes Magazine* rated her at number 76 on their 2005 power in entertainment list.

Naomi Watts has maintained privacy in her personal life. She dated fellow actor Heath Ledger from 2002 till May 2004. She believes in living her life in dignity and is happy that she is often not recognized in public. For a girl who decided to become an actress after seeing the movie *Fame,* she has come a long way.

Kate Winslet

BIRTH NAME Kate Elizabeth Winslet
BORN October 5, 1975
DROPPED OUT Middle School

KATE WINSLET WAS born in Reading, England, in 1975. Her family has a long history in the theatre. Her parents, Roger Winslet and Sally Bridges-Winslet are both accomplished actors; her maternal grandparents, Oliver and Linda Bridges, ran the Reading Repertory Theatre. Kate has two sisters, Anna and Beth, both of whom are involved in the theatre, and one brother, Joss.

Surrounded by theatre, Kate realized her interest lay in acting, and she began performing early on. She took whatever roles came her way as a child and was focused on achieving her goals. When she was 11, she convinced her father to send her to Redroofs Theatre School in Maidenhead. It was an exclusive school, with children from rich families; Kate, who was not wealthy and was often teased for her weight, felt an outsider.

At 13, Kate appeared on television in episodes of *Shrinks* and *Casualty*. In a role in *Dark Season*, in 1991, she met and dated Stephen Tredre, 12 years older, for almost five years. In 1994 at the age of 18 she was excited to earn a part in *Heavenly Creatures*.

In 1995, Winslet was nominated for an Oscar for her role in *Sense and Sensibility*, and she won a BAFTA for it. The next year, she played the title role in *Jude* and *Ophelia* in Hamlet. It was, however, her role as Rose DeWitt Bukater in *Titanic* that made her an international star overnight. She was again nominated for an Academy Award, making her the youngest actress to be nominated twice.

Titanic was the most successful movie of all time and Winslett couldn't have asked for a better launching pad. Surprisingly, she did not accept offers for roles in prestigious projects like *Shakespeare in Love* and *The King and I*. She worked instead on smaller, independent films like *Hideous Kinky, Holy Smoke* and *Quills,* in which she played chambermaid to Marquis de Sade.

Since 2001, Winslet has acted in *Iris,* with Dame Judi Dench, *Enigma, The Life of David Gale, Finding Neverland,* with Johnny Depp, and *Eternal Sunshine of the Spotless Mind,* with Jim Carrey. For the latter two movies she was nominated for best actress awards—a BAFTA for *Finding Neverland* and an Oscar for *Eternal Sunshine of the Spotless Mind*—but did not win either.

Winslet is a fiercely independent woman, accepting only those roles she strongly believes in. Though she became anorexic in reaction to the teasing she received as a child, she has been outspoken about her refusal to lose weight in order to conform to the Hollywood ideal. In 2003 the editor of *GQ* took the liberty of airbrushing some photos to make her look dramatically thinner than she actually was. She came forward and issued a statement saying that the alterations were made without her consent.

Kate Winslet's hometown of Reading has named a street in her honor, Winslet Place, near the site of a demolished cinema.

Catherine Zeta-Jones

BIRTH NAME Catherine Jones

BORN September 25, 1969

DROPPED OUT Dumbarton School

CATHERINE JONES WAS born in Swansea, Wales, and grew up in the seaside town of Mumbles, where her father, Dai Jones, worked as a manager at a candy factory. Her chosen name honors her grandmothers, Catherine Fair and Zeta Jones. Catherine has two brothers, David, who is an executive with the Initial Entertainment Group, and Lyndon, who is her business manager.

Interested in acting from an early age, Catherine was part of her church congregation's troupe. Her first stage production was in Annie, when she was 10. At 14, she was spotted by Monkees star Micky Dolenz and landed parts in *The Pajama Game* and *42nd Street*. When she was 15, Catherine dropped out of Dumbarton School in Swansea so she could concentrate on her acting career and travel for performances. Catherine's next was the West End production of *Bugsy Malone*. Her first movie was the low budget *Scheherazade*, after which she appeared on television in *The Darling Buds of May*, *Christopher Columbus: The Discovery* and *Splitting Heirs*.

With the fame brought by *The Darling Buds of May*, Zeta-Jones was a successful star in the U.K., long before the U.S. audience had even heard of her. Steven Spielberg noticed her performance in the Lifetime Television series *Titanic* and recommended her for *The Mask of Zorro*. The movie was a huge hit; it shot Zeta-Jones to international stardom and made her part of the top league in Hollywood.

Zeta-Jones has worked with the most famous actors in Hollywood and has been part of several blockbusters, including *Entrapment*, *The Haunting*, *Traffic*, *The Terminal*, *Intolerable Cruelty*, *America's Sweethearts*, *High Fidelity* and *Ocean's Twelve*.

Her career-defining role came in 2003 in the hit musical *Chicago*.

Co-starring with Richard Gere and Renée Zellweger, Zeta-Jones danced and performed her own songs, showcasing her incredible talent. Her scintillating performance in the movie, as Velma Kelly, won her an Academy Award for best supporting actress in 2003 and a nomination for the Golden Globes.

Zeta-Jones met Michael Douglas in Deauville, France, on a promotional tour for *The Mask of Zorro*. They were married in November 2000. They have two children, a son Dylan, born in 2000, and a daughter, Carys, born in 2003. Proud of her Welsh heritage and determined to teach her children about their history, Zeta-Jones has built a home in Swansea.

Zeta-Jones is known for her spunk as well as her femininity and has been featured on best-dressed lists regularly. She is currently the spokesperson and model for Elizabeth Arden Cosmetics. A strong-willed and independent woman, she is passionate about what she does in life, whether it is her acting work or raising her children or anything else she undertakes. Zeta-Jones is also an accomplished golfer and was on the winning European team of The All Star Cup, held in August 2005.

Your Personal Biography

Your Personal Biography

Your Personal Biography

Your Personal Biography

Your Personal Biography

Your Personal Biography

Your Personal Biography

Your Personal Biography

Your Personal Biography

Your Name_____

BIRTH NAME _____

BORN _____

DROPPED OUT _____

_____

_____

_____

_____

_____

_____

_____

_____

_____

_____

_____

FAME_____ NAME_____

Appendix

Here is a list of some prominent dropouts in many fields. They did not all achieve great wealth; many achieved greatness in other ways. All of them have fascinating life stories, though.

I've included just a few words about each person to remind you of why you might have heard of them.

Name	Reminder	Dropped Out
	The World of Business	
	Billionaires	
Roman Abramovich	Oil	College
Sheldon Adelson	Casinos, hotels	College
Paul Allen	Microsoft	College
Herbert Allen Jr.	Investment banker	High school
Dhirubhai Ambani	Reliance Group—textiles	High school
Micky Arison	Carnival Cruise Line	High school
Steven Ballmer	Microsoft	College
Bill Bartman	Wall Street—filed bankruptcy twice	High school
Richard Branson	Virgin Enterprises	High school
James Cayne	Bear Stearns	College
Jim Clark	Netscape	High school
Jack Cooke	Broadcasting	High school
Constantino De Oliveira Jr.	Airline entrepreneur	College
Michael Dell	Dell Computers	College
Richard Desmond	British newspaper publisher	High school
Barry Diller	Television executive	College
Charles Dolan	Cablevision Systems	College
Larry Ellison	Oracle	College
David Filo	Yahoo!	College
Thomas Flatley	Real estate	College
Sidney Frank	Grey Goose vodka	College
Yoshitaka Fukuda	Credit banking	High school
Bill Gates	Microsoft	College
David Geffen	Dreamworks SKG	College
Alan Gerry	Cablevision	High school
Lim Goh Tong	Gaming	High school
Thomas Haffa	Media	High school
Kenneth Hendricks	Building supplies	High school
Stanley Ho	Gaming	College
H. Wayne Huizenga	Blockbuster Video, team owner	College
H.L. Hunt	Oil industrialist	Elementary school

Name	Reminder	Dropped Out
\multicolumn{3}{c}{The World of Business (*continued*)}		

The World of Business (*continued*)

Billionaires (*continued*)

Name	Reminder	Dropped Out
Carl Icahn	Corporate raider	College
James Jannard	Oakley sunglasses	College
Steve Jobs	Apple Computer	College
Li Ka-shing	Investor	High school
Kirk Kerkorian	Investor	High school
Ray Kroc	McDonald's	High school
Ralph Lauren	Polo	College
Joe Lewis	Investor	High school
Richard Li	Telecom	College
Carl Lindner Jr.	American Financial Group	High school
Robert Maxwell	Publisher	High school
William Morean	Jabil Circuit	College
David H. Murdock	CEO Dole Foods	High school
Donald Newhouse	Publisher	College
Amancio Ortega	Apparel	High school
Gregorio Perez	Oil and gas	High school
John D. Rockefeller	Standard Oil	High school
Winthrop Rockefeller	Banking	College
Kjell Inge Rokke	Industrialist	High school
Phillip Ruffin	Casino, real estate	College
Edmond Safra	Banking	High school
Yasumitsu Shigeta	Telecom	College
J.R. Simplot	French fries	High school
Daniel Snyder	Sports team owner	College
Sheldon Solow	Real estate	College
Steven Spielberg	*E.T., Indiana Jones;* Oscar winner	College
A. Alfred Taubman	Real estate	College
Jack Taylor	Enterprise Rent-A-Car	College
Ted Turner	Media mogul	College
Donald John Tyson	Tyson Foods	College
Albert Ueltschi	Flight safety training school	College
Theodore Waitt	Gateway	College
Ty Warner	Ty Beanie Babies	College
Hiroshi Yamauchi	Nintendo Corporation	College
Jerry Yang	Yahoo!	College
Ahmet Zorlu	Electronics	High school

Millionaires

Name	Reminder	Dropped Out
John Jacob Astor	America's first millionaire	High school
Asa Candler	Coca-Cola pioneer	College
Kevin Cannon	Freight Software	College
Andrew Carnegie	Legacy	Elementary school
Charles E. Culpeper	Coca Cola bottler	High school
Thomas Gallagher	Vice-president CIBC Oppenheimer	College
Richard Grasso	New York Stock Exchange	College
Kevin Liles	Warner Music Group, Def Jam	College
Del E. Webb	Developer; Yankees owner	High school

Name	Reminder	Dropped Out
The World of Business (COntinued)		
Company Founders		
Wally Amos	Famous Amos Cookies	High school
Walter Anderson	White Castle Hamburger	College
Anne Beiler	Auntie Anne's	High school
Joe Biedenharn	Coca-Cola Bottling	High school
William Boeing	Boeing Aircraft	College
Milton Bradley	Toys	College
Dov Charney	American Apparel	College
Ben Cohen	Ben & Jerry's Ice Cream	College
Harry Cohn	Columbia Pictures	High school
Joshua Lionel Cowen	Lionel Trains	College
Jimmy Dean	Jimmy Dean Foods	High school
Xavier Delacour	Attune LLC	High school
Walt Disney	Disney Studios	High school
Charles Dow	Dow Jones	High school
Matt Drudge	Drudge Report	High school
George Eastman	Eastman Kodak	High school
Max Factor	Max Factor cosmetics	Elementary school
Shawn Fanning	Napster	College
Henry Ford	Ford Motor Company	High school
Patrick Frawley	Papermate Pens	High school
James Gamble	Procter & Gamble	High school
Amadeo Peter Giannini	Bank of America	High school
King Gillette	Gillette razors	High school
Berry Gordy	Motown Records	High school
Florence Graham	Elizabeth Arden cosmetics	College
W.T. Grant	W.T. Grant Stores	High school
Horace Greeley	*New York Tribune;* U.S. Congress	High school
Ruth Handler	Mattel; Barbie Doll	College
Fred Harvey	Harvey House restaurants	High school
Milton Hershey	Hershey Chocolate	Elementary school
Soichiro Honda	Honda	High school
John H Johnson	Ebony, Jet magazines	College
Kenneth Johnson	Dial-A-Waiter	College
Edward Jones	Dow Jones	College
Henry J. Kaiser	Kaiser Aluminum	High school
Edwin H. Land	Polaroid	College
Marcus Loew	MGM; Loews Theatres	High school
Mary Lyon	Mount Holyoke College	High school
John Mackey	Whole Foods	College
Frank Mars	Mars Candy	High school
Tom Monaghan	Domino's Pizza	College
Eric Morley	Miss World Pageant	High school
Christopher Morrison	PLPDigital Systems	College
David Neelman	Jet Blue	College
Mary Pickford	United Artists	High school
Joseph Pulitzer	*New York World*	High school
Bill Rosenberg	Dunkin' Donuts	High school

Name	Reminder	Dropped Out
	The World of Business (continued)	
	Company Founders (continued)	
Harold Ross	*The New Yorker*	High school
Frederick Henry Royce	Rolls Royce	Elementary school
Rick Rubin	Def Jam Records	College
Harland Sanders	Kentucky Fried Chicken	Elementary school
Margaret Sanger	American Birth Control League	College
David Sarnoff	RCA, NBC	High school
Vidal Sassoon	Vidal Sassoon Hair Products	High school
W. Clement Stone	*Success Magazine*	Elementary school
Alan Sugar	Amstrad	High school
Dave Thomas	Wendy's	High school
Jann Wenner	*Rolling Stone*	College
George Westinghouse	Westinghouse Electric Company	College
Kemmons Wilson	Holiday Inn	High school
Steve Wozniak	Apple Computer	College
William Wrigley Jr.	Wrigley's Gum	High school
	Entrepreneurs	
John Barfield	The Bartech Group	High school
Carl G. Fisher	Developer	Elementary school
Freddie Laker	Airline	High school
David Martin	Martin Zambito Art Gallery	High school
Frank McKinney	Builder	College
Mary & Kate Olsen	Olsen twins	College
Tim Paulson	Writer, coach	College
Stanley Perron	Real estate, Australia's ninth richest man	High school
Muriel Siebert	First woman member, NYSE	College
Dawn Steel	Columbia Pictures	College
Ryan Tewis	Real estate	College
Travis Tollestrup	Real estate	College
Charles Urban	Movie theatres	High school
Jimmie Wedell	Aviation school owner	College
Dave Woodward	Marketing guru	College
Frank Woodward	Jell-O	High school
Woody Woodward	Sold first idea at age 16	High school
Dominick Zambito	Martin Zambito Art Gallery	High school
Adolph Zukor	Paramount Pictures	High school
	Executives	
R.J. Funkhouser	Banker	Elementary school
Wayne Inouye	Gateway Computers	College
Allen W. Jacobson	Boeing manager	High school
Harry Winston	Jeweler	High school
	The World of Technology	
	Scientists and Engineers	
Herbert Brown	Chemist	High school
Albert Einstein	Physicist	High school

Name	Reminder	Dropped Out
	The World of Technology (*continued*)	

Name	Reminder	Dropped Out
	Scientists and Engineers (continued)	
Michael Faraday	Physicist	High school
Oliver Heaviside	Applied mathematician	High school
Jaron Lanier	Computer scientist; virtual reality pioneer	High school
Arthur Ernest Morgan	Flood control engineer	High school
Valentina Tereshkova	Cosmonaut, first woman in space	High school
Anton van Leeuwenhok	Microscope maker; discovered bacteria	High school
Frank Lloyd Wright	Architect	College
	Inventors	
Ole Kirk Christian	Legos	Elementary school
James B. Eads	Steel-arch bridge	High school
Thomas Edison	Over 2,000 patents	Elementary school
Oliver Evans	Steam engine	High school
Philo T. Farnsworth	Television	College
Chester Greenwood	Earmuffs	Elementary school
Frederick Jones	Refrigerated truck	High school
Dean Kamen	Segway	College
Gordon Langford	Flexpoint sensor	College
William Lear	Learjet	High school
Adolph Levis	Slim Jim	High school
Guglielmo Marconi	Wireless telegraphy (radio)	Elementary school
Hiram Maxim	Machine-gun	High school
Elijah McCoy	Automatic lubricator; ironing board	High school
Florence Melton	Foam slippers	High school
Garrett Morgan	Traffic signal; gas mask; protective gear	High school
Earl Muntz	Car stereo tape deck; affordable TV set	High school
James Naismith	Basketball	High school
Isaac Merrit Singer	Practical sewing machine	Elementary school
Nikola Tesla	Radio	High school
C.J. Walker	Hair products	Elementary school
Orville Wright	Airplane	High school
Wilbur Wright	Airplane	High school
	The Media	
	Publishers	
Felix Dennis	*Maxim Magazine*	High school
Jimmy Lai	Hong Kong media tycoon	Elementary school
Adolph Ochs	*New York Times*	High school
Henry Parks	Australian newspaper publisher, politician	High school
Lyle Stuart	Publisher of controversial books	High school
	Editors	
Mortimer Adler	*Encyclopedia Britannica*	High school
Walter Anderson	*Parade*	High school
Karl Hess	*Newsweek*	High school
Diana Vreeland	Fashion magazines	High school

Name	Reminder	Dropped Out
	The Media (continued)	
	Journalists	
Tucker Carlson	*Crossfire*	College
John Chancellor	*NBC Nightly News*	High school
Walter Cronkite	CBS News	College
Pete Hamill	*New York Post*	High school
Peter Jennings	*ABC World News Tonight*	High school
Matt Lauer	*Today Show*	College
Andrea Thompson	*CNN Headline News*	High school
Nina Totenberg	National Public Radio	College
	Television Personalities	
Simon Cowell	*American Idol* judge, music producer	High school
Bill Cullen	Game show host	High school
Carson Daly	Talk show host	College
Jenny Jones	Talk show host	High school
Lisa Ling	Talk show host	College
Frank Nicotero	Game show host	College
Jack Paar	Talk show host	High school
Lawrence Welk	TV bandleader	High school
	Radio Personalities	
Art Bell	Hosts paranormal-themed shows	High school
Don Imus	*Imus in the Morning*	High school
Wolfman Jack	Top 40 rock and roll pioneer	High school
Rush Limbaugh	Talk show host	College
Ron Reagan Jr.	Political commentator	College
	Society at Large	
	Academics	
Daniel Gilbert	Harvard psychology professor	High school
Hubert Bancroft	Historian	High school
Walter L. Smith	President, Florida A&M University	High school
	Social Activists	
Brooke Astor	Philanthropist	High school
Erin Brockovich	Environmental activist	High school
Margaret Brown	Philanthropist, Titanic survivor	High school
Cesar Chavez	Farmworker rights activist	High school
Diana, Princess of Wales	Philanthropist	High school
Samuel Gompers	Labor rights activist	Elementary school
John Llewellyn	Labor rights activist	High school
Florence Nightingale	Nursing pioneer	High school
Rosa Parks	Civil rights activist	High school
Oral Roberts	Evangelist	High school
Malcolm X	Civil rights activist	High school
	Popular Culture Notables	
Daniel Boone	Frontiersman	High school
Gisele Bündchen	Model	High school

Millionaire Dropouts

Name	Reminder	Dropped Out
	Society at Large (*continued*)	
	Popular Culture Notables (*continued*)	
Brooke Burke	Model; TV host	College
Jackie Cochran	Aviation pioneer	Elementary school
William Cody	*Buffalo Bill's Wild West Show*	Elementary school
Christopher Columbus	Explorer	High school
James Cook	Explorer	High school
Cindy Crawford	Model	College
Davy Crockett	Frontiersman, Congressman	High school
Heidi Dinan	Mrs. America 2004	College
Elizabeth Jagger	Model	High school
Evel Knievel	Daredevil	High school
Henrietta Leaver	Model; Miss America 1935	High school
Audrey Marnay	Model	High school
Jenny McCarthy	Model, actress, MTV host	College
Heather Mills	Model; anti-land mine activist	High school
Annie Oakley	Sharpshooter; entertainer	High school
Philippe Petit	High wire performer	High school
Sam Phillips	Rock and roll pioneer	High school
Paulina Porizkova	Model	High school
Eddie Rickenbacker	World War I flying ace	High school
Will Rogers	Humorist	High school
Rebecca Romijn-Stamos	Model	College
Robert F. Scott	Explorer	High school
Molly Sims	Model	College
Henry Stanley	Explorer	High school
	Politicians and Statesmen	
Cruz Bustamante	California lieutenant governor	College
Ben Nighthorse Cambell	U.S. senator	High school
Richard Carmona	U.S. surgeon general	High school
Grover Cleveland	U.S. president	High school
James Farley	Postmaster general under FDR	Elementary school
Millard Fillmore	U.S. president	Elementary school
James Florio	New Jersey governor 1990–1994	High school
Benjamin Franklin	Printer, inventor, statesman	High school
Mohandes Gandhi	Indian independence leader	High school
Barry Goldwater	U.S. senator	College
Roy Greensmith	Sheriff of Nottingham, U.K., 1995–1996	High school
William Henry Harrison	U.S. president	High school
Arthur Henderson	Co-founder of Britain's Labor Party	High school
Patrick Henry	Virginia's first governor	Elementary school
Andrew Jackson	U.S. president	High school
Andrew Johnson	U.S. president	High school
John Paul Jones	Naval commander	High school
Leon Jouhaux	French labor leader	High school
Bernard Kerik	New York police commissioner	High school
Abraham Lincoln	U.S. president	Elementary school

Name	Reminder	Dropped Out
Society at Large (*continued*)		
Politicians and Statesmen (*continued*)		
John Major	British prime minister 1990–1997	High school
Thomas Maltby	Australian political leader	High school
Mike Mansfield	U.S. senator	High school
William McKinley	U.S. president	College
Melina Mercouri	Greek politician; actress	High school
Ruth Ann Minner	Delaware governor 2001–2005	High school
Joseph Moakley	U.S. congressman	High school
James Monroe	U.S. president	College
Walter Nash	New Zealand prime minister, 1957–1960	High school
Evita Peron	Argentinian political leader	High school
Charles Rangel	U.S. congressman	High school
James E. Rogan	U.S. congressman	High school
Karl Rove	White House senior advisor	College
Arnold Schwarzenegger	Governor of California	High school
Alfred Smith	New York governor, 1928 presidential nominee	Elementary school
Zachary Taylor	U.S. president	High school
Harry Truman	U.S. president	College
Martin Van Buren	U.S. president	High school
Antonio Villaraigosa	Mayor of Los Angeles	High school
George Washington	U.S. president	High school
The Fine Arts		
Writers		
Hans Christian Andersen	Children's stories	High school
Jane Austen	*Pride and Prejudice*	Elementary school
John Bartlett	*Bartlett's Familiar Quotations*	High school
Barbara Taylor Bradford	Romance novels	High school
Rick Bragg	*Ava's Man*	College
Hall Caines	*The Christian*	Elementary school
Albert Camus	*The Plague*	High school
Truman Capote	*Breakfast at Tiffany's*	High school
Raymond Chandler	Noir detective novels	College
G. K. Chesterton	*The Man Who Was Thursday*	College
Agatha Christie	*Death on the Nile*	Elementary school
Samuel L. Clemens	*Tom Sawyer*	Elementary school
Jackie Collins	*Hollywood Husbands*	High school
Joseph Conrad	*Heart of Darkness*	High school
Lloyd Dennis	*His Way Works*	High school
Charles Dickens	*A Christmas Carol*	Elementary school
James Dickey	*Deliverance*	High school
James Ellroy	*L.A. Confidential*	High school
Howard Fast	*Spartacus*	High school
William Faulkner	*The Sound and the Fury*	High school
F Scott Fitzgerald	*The Great Gatsby*	College
Shelby Foote	*The Civil War*	College
Henry George	*Progress and Poverty*	Elementary school

Name	Reminder	Dropped Out
\multicolumn{3}{c}{The Fine Arts (*continued*)}		

The Fine Arts (*continued*)

Writers (continued)

Name	Reminder	Dropped Out
Alex Haley	*Roots*	High school
Eric Hoffer	*The True Believer*	High school
Louis L'Amour	Westerns	High school
Fran Lebowitz	*Metropolitan Life*	High school
Doris Lessing	*Children of Violence*	High school
Jack London	*Call of the Wild*	High school
Richard Marcinko	*Rogue Warrior*	High school
Harry Martinson	*Wild Bouquet*	High school
Moa Martinson	*My Mother Gets Married*	High school
Oseola McCarty	*Riches of Oseola McCarty*	Elementary school
Herman Melville	*Moby-Dick*	High school
Dave Pelzer	*The Privilege of Youth*	High school
Edgar Allen Poe	Horror stories, poetry	College
Harold Robbins	*The Carpetbaggers*	High school
Nora Roberts	*Naked in Death*	High school
J.D. Salinger	*The Catcher In the Rye*	College
Carl Sandburg	*Abraham Lincoln*	High school
José Saramago	*Baltasar and Blimunda*	High school
John Steinbeck	*The Grapes of Wrath*	High school
Leo Tolstoy	*War and Peace*	College
H.G. Wells	*War of the Worlds*	High school
Richard Wright	*Native Son*	High school

Poets

Name	Reminder	Dropped Out
Maya Angelou	*The Heart of a Woman*	College
William Blake	*Songs of Innocence*	High school
Joseph Brodsky	*A Part of Speech*	High school
John Clare	*The Rural Muse*	High school
Robert Frost	*In the Clearing*	Elementary school
Langston Hughes	*Shakespeare in Harlem*	College
Gwendolyn MacEwen	*The Fire-Eaters*	High school
Rod McKuen	*Listen to the Warm*	Elementary school
Banjo Paterson	Australian bush poet, "Waltzing Matilda"	High school
Alexander Pope	*The Rape of the Lock*	High school
Patti Smith	*Auguries of Innocence*	College
Ron Whitehead	*I Will Not Bow Down*	High school
Walt Whitman	*Leaves of Grass*	Elementary school

Composers and Songwriters

Name	Reminder	Dropped Out
Peter Allen	"I Go To Rio"	High school
Gene Autry	"Here Comes Santa Claus"	High school
Irving Berlin	"White Christmas"	High school
Jacques Brel	Belgian actor, author, composer, poet	High school
Sammy Cahn	"High Hopes"	High school
Jim Dale	"Georgy Girl"	High school
Thomas Dolby	"She Blinded Me with Science "	High school
Duke Ellington	"Black, Brown and Beige"	High school

Name	Reminder	Dropped Out
	**The Fine Arts** (*continued*)	

Composers and Songwriters (*continued*)

Name	Reminder	Dropped Out
George Gershwin	*Rhapsody in Blue*	High school
Burton Lane	"How are Things in Glocca Morra?"	High school
Oscar Levant	Broadway and Hollywood composer	High school
John Philip Sousa	"Stars and Stripes Forever"	Elementary school
Andrew Lloyd Webber	*The Phantom of the Opera, Evita, Cats*	College
John Zorn	Avant-garde composer	College

Playwrights and Screen Writers

Name	Reminder	Dropped Out
Edward Albee	*Who's Afraid of Virginia Woolf?*	College
Sean O'Casey	*The Plough and the Stars*	Elementary school
John Fusco	*Hidalgo*	High school
Garson Kanin	*Born Yesterday*	High achool
Elaine May	*A New Leaf*	High achool
Tim Rice	Lyricist, *Jesus Christ, Superstar; The Lion King*	College
William Saroyan	*The Time of Your Life*	High achool
William Shakespeare	*Romeo and Juliet*	High school
George Bernard Shaw	*Pygmalion*	High school
Tennessee Williams	*Cat on a Hot Tin Roof*	College
August Wilson	*Ma Rainey's Black Bottom*	High school

Artists

Name	Reminder	Dropped Out
Edwin Apps	*Fishers of Men*	High school
James Flagg	Illustrator; "I Want You for the U.S. Army" poster	High school
Claude Monet	*Water Lilies*	Elementary school
LeRoy Neiman	Sports and jazz portraits	High school
Yoko Ono	Performance art, conceptual art	College
Lesser Ury	*City Lights*	High school
Vincent Van Gogh	*Starry Night*	High school

Photographers and Sculptors

Name	Reminder	Dropped Out
Ansel Adams	Wilderness photographer	High school
Richard Avedon	Fashion and portrait photographer	High school
Helmut Newton	Fashion and figure photographer	High school
Gordon Parks	*Life* magazine photographer; polymath	High school
Edward Leedskalnin	Sculptor, *Coral Castle* in Homestead, Florida	Elementary school

Fashion Designers

Name	Reminder	Dropped Out
Miguel Adrover	Avant-garde designer	High school
Liz Claiborne	Liz Claiborne, Inc.	High school
Tom Ford	Gucci	College
Alexander McQueen	Givenchy	High school
Gloria Vanderbilt	Designer jeans	High school

Filmmakers

Name	Reminder	Dropped Out
Woody Allen	*Annie Hall*	College
Paul Anderson	*Boogie Nights*	High school
Peter Bogdanovich	*Mask*	High school
John Boorman	*The Tailor of Panama*	High school

Name	Reminder	Dropped Out

Name | *Reminder* | *Dropped Out*

The Fine Arts (*continued*)

Filmmakers (*continued*)

Name	Reminder	Dropped Out
Stan Brakhage	*Work in Progress*	College
James Cameron	*Titanic*	College
Robert Evans	*Chinatown*	High school
Samuel Fuller	*The Day of Reckoning*	High school
Lew Grade	*The Muppet Movie*	High school
D.W. Griffith	*Birth of a Nation*	High school
William Hanna	Animator, Hanna–Barbera Productions	College
John Huston	*The Maltese Falcon*	High school
Peter Jackson	*Lord of the Rings*	High school
Stanley Kubrick	*2001: A Space Odyssey*	High school
David Lean	*Dr. Zhivago*	High school
Joseph Levine	*The Graduate*	High school
Michael Moore	*Fahrenheit 9/11*	High school
Jon Peters	*The Color Purple*	Elementary school
David Puttman	*Chariots of Fire*	High school
Guy Ritchie	*Swept Away*	High school
Kevin Smith	*Clerks*	College
Robert Stigwood	*Saturday Night Fever*	High school
Quentin Tarantino	*Pulp Fiction*	High school
François Truffaut	*The 400 Blows*	High school
John Woo	*Broken Arrow*	High school

The Performing Arts

Dancers

Name	Reminder	Dropped Out
Josephine Baker	U.S. expatriate star in Europe	High school
Isadora Duncan	Mother of modern dance	Elementary school
Lola Falana	U.S. dancer, actress	High school
Bill "Bojangles" Robinson	U.S. tap dancer	Elementary school

Musicians and Singers

Name	Reminder	Dropped Out
Bryan Adams	Canadian singer–songwriter	High school
Christina Aguilera	U.S. singer–songwriter	High school
Rick Allen	Def Leppard drummer	High school
Joan Armatrading	U.K. singer–songwriter	High school
Louis Armstrong	Jazz trumpeter, singer	High school
Eddy Arnold	Country music singer	High school
Chet Atkins	Country music guitarist	High school
Pearl Bailey	U.S. singer	High school
Shirley Bassey	Welsh singer	High school
Beck	U.S. musician	High school
André Benjamin	Rapper André 3000 of OutKast	High school
Chuck Berry	Rock pioneer; singer–composer	High school
Mary J. Blige	U.S. singer–songwriter	High school
Clint Black	Country singer–songwriter	High school
Norman Blake	U.S. songwriter–musician	High school
Michael Bolton	U.S. singer–songwriter	High school
Sonny Bono	U.S. singer, producer, politician	High school

Name	Reminder	Dropped Out
	The Performing Arts (*continued*)	
	Musicians and Singers (*continued*)	
David Bowie	U.K. singer, musician, writer	High school
Billy Bragg	U.K. folk and protest musician	High school
Gary Brooker	Procol Harum pianist, singer–songwriter	High school
Pete Burns	U.K. singer–songwriter	Elementary school
David Byrne	Talking Heads songwriter	College
Glen Campbell	Country singer	High school
Viki Carr	U.S. singer	High school
Ray Charles	U.S. pianist–singer	High school
Cher	U.S. singer, actress	High school
Eric Clapton	U.K. guitarist, composer, singer	High school
Kurt Cobain	Nirvana singer–songwriter	High school Eddie
Cochran	U.S. rockabilly musician	High school
Joe Cocker	U.K. rock and blues musician	High school
Phil Collins	Genesis lead singer, drummer	High school
Russ Conway	U.K. pianist	High school
Perry Como	U.S. crooner	High school
Elvis Costello	U.K. singer–songwriter	High school
Roger Daltry	Lead singer, The Who	High school
Vic Damone	U.S. singer	High school
Sammy Davis Jr.	U.S. singer, dancer, comedian, actor	Elementary school
Neil Diamond	U.S. singer	College
Bo Diddley	U.S. singer–songwriter	High school
Celine Dion	Canadian pop singer	High school
Steve Earle	Country singer–songwriter	High school
Eminem	Rap artist	High school
Adam Faith	U.K. singer, actor	High school
Perry Farrell	U.S. alternative rock musician	College
José Feliciano	Puerto Rican singer	High school
Ella Fitzgerald	U.S. jazz singer	High school
Peter Frampton	U.K. rock musician	High school
Aretha Franklin	U.S. singer	High school
Jerry Garcia	Grateful Dead guitarist, lead singer	High school
Mary Gauthier	U.S. folksinger–songwriter	High school
Marvin Gaye	U.S. singer–songwriter, producer	High school
Boy George	Culture Club singer–songwriter	High school
Andy Gibb	U.K.–Australian singer	Elementary school
Barry Gibb	U.K. singer–songwriter, the Bee Gees	High school
Maurice Gibb	U.K. musician, the Bee Gees	High school
Robin Gibb	U.K. singer, the Bee Gees	High school
Dizzy Gillespie	Jazz trumpeter	High school
Benny Goodman	U.S. clarinetist, swing bandleader	High school
Graham Gouldman	U.K. songwriter, bass player	High school
Josh Groban	U.S. singer–songwriter	College
Dave Grohl	Nirvana , Foo Fighters drummer	High school
Arlo Guthrie	U.S. folksinger–songwriter	College
Woody Guthrie	U.S. folksinger–songwriter	High school
Merle Haggard	U.S. singer–songwriter	High school

Name	Reminder	Dropped Out
	The Performing Arts (continued)	
	Musicians and Singers (continued)	
Bill Haley	U.S. rock and roll pioneer	High school
Jet Harris	Bass guitarist, The Shadows	High school
George Harrison	Beatles singer–songwriter	High school
Beth Hart	U.S. singer	High school
Jimi Hocking	U.S. singer–songwriter	High school
Billie Holiday	U.S. jazz singer	Elementary school
John Lee Hooker	U.S. singer–songwriter	High school
Fiona Horne	Australian singer	High school
Lena Horne	U.S. singer	High school
Janis Ian	U.S. singer–songwriter	High school
Enrique Iglesias	Spanish singer	College
Natalie Imbruglia	Australian singer, actress	High school
Burl Ives	U.S. folk singer	College
LL Cool J	Rap artist	High school
Waylon Jennings	U.S. singer, guitarist	High school
Joan Jett	U.S. singer, guitarist	High school
Billy Joel	U.S. singer–songwriter, pianist	High school
George Jones	U.S. country singer	Elementary school
Norah Jones	U.S. singer–songwriter, pianist	College
Rickie Lee Jones	U.S. singer–songwriter	High school
Tom Jones	Welsh pop singer	High school
Joshua Kadison	U.S. rock pianist–composer	High school
Chaka Khan	U.S. singer	High school
B.B. King	U.S. singer–songwriter, blues guitarist	High school
Gladys Knight	U.S. singer, actress	High school
J. Fred Knobloch	U.S. singer–songwriter	High school
Cleo Laine	U.K. jazz singer	High school
Cyndi Lauper	U.S. pop singer, actress	High school
Avril Lavigne	Canadian singer–songwriter, actress	High school
Steve Lawrence	U.S. singer, actor	High school
Albert Lee	U.K. guitarist	High school
Sean Lennon	U.S. musician	College
Huey Lewis	U.S. singer, musician	College
Jerry Lee Lewis	U.S. singer–songwriter, pianist	High school
Mark Lindsay	Paul Revere and the Raiders lead singer	High school
Brian Littrell	U.S. singer, member of Backstreet Boys	High school
David Lon	U.S. musician	High school
Julie London	U.S. singer, actress	High school
Trini Lopez	U.S. singer, guitarist	High school
Courtney Love	U.S. singer, actress	High school
Loretta Lynn	U.S. country singer	High school
Shelby Lynne	U.S. singer–songwriter	High school
Madonna	U.S. singer–songwriter, actress, author	College
Shirley Manson	Scottish musician, singer	High school
Dean Martin	U.S. singer, actor	High school
John Mayer	U.S. singer–songwriter	College
Natalie Merchant	U.S. singer–songwriter	High school

Appendix

Name	Reminder	Dropped Out
The Performing Arts (*continued*)		
Musicians and Singers (continued)		
George Michael	U.K. singer–songwriter	High school
Roger Miller	U.S. singer–songwriter	Elementary school
Steve Miller	U.S. guitarist	College
Liza Minnelli	U.S. singer, actress	High school
Bill Monroe	U.S. singer, composer, bandleader	Elementary school
John Michael Montgomery	U.S. country singer	High school
John Mooney	U.S. blues guitarist	High school
Van Morrison	Irish singer–songwriter	High school
Samantha Mumba	Irish pop singer, actress	High school
Nelly	Rap artist	High school
Willie Nelson	U.S. singer–songwriter	College
Wayne Newton	U.S. pop singer	High school
Olivia Newton-John	Australian singer, actress	High school
Sinéad O'Connor	Irish singer–songwriter	High school
Gil Ofarim	German singer–songwriter, actor	High school
Kelly Osbourne	U.K. singer, actress, fashion designer	High school
Ozzy Osbourne	U.K. singer	High school
Jimmy Page	U.K. rock guitarist	High school
Charlie Parker	U.S. jazz saxophonist	High school
Neil Peart	Canadian drummer, lyricist	High school
Tom Petty	U.S. singer–songwriter	High school
Pink	U.S. singer–songwriter	High school
Charley Pride	U.S. country singer	High school
Prince	U.S. singer–songwriter	High school
Otis Redding	U.S. singer	High school
Lou Reed	U.S. singer–songwriter	College
J.J. Reneaux	U.S. singer–songwriter, author	High school
Paul Revere	U.S. rock organist	High school
Trent Reznor	U.S. singer–songwriter	College
Charlie Rich	U.S. blues singer	College
Busta Rhymes	Rap artist	High school
Kid Rock	Rap artist	High school
Axl Rose	U.S. singer–songwriter	High school
Ja Rule	Rap artist	High school
Seal	U.K. soul singer	High school
Pete Seeger	U.S. folk singer	College
Frank Sinatra	U.S. pop singer	High school
Sammi Smith	U.S. country singer	High school
Scott Stapp	U.S. singer–songwriter	High school
Ringo Starr	U.K. rock drummer, singer	High school
Donna Summer	U.S. pop singer	High school
James Taylor	U.S. singer–songwriter	High school
Koko Taylor	U.S. blues singer	Elementary school
Rob Thomas	U.S. pop singer	High school
Cyndi Thomson	U.S. country singer	College
Jeff Timmons	U.S. pop singer	College
Randy Travis	U.S. country singer	High school

Name	Reminder	Dropped Out
	The Performing Arts (*continued*)	
	Musicians and Singers (*continued*)	
Robin Trower	U.K. rock guitarist	High school
Tanya Tucker	U.S. country singer	High school
Steven Tyler	U.S. singer–songwriter	High school
Stevie Ray Vaughan	U.S. blues guitarist	High school
Eddie Vedder	U.S. singer	High school
Sid Vicious	U.K. rock musician	High school
Eddie Walker	U.K. singer–songwriter	High school
Steve Waller	U.K. singer, guitarist	High school
Doc Watson	U.S. singer–songwriter	Elementary school
Kitty Wells	U.S. country singer	High school
Kanye West	Rap artist	College
Barry White	U.S. pop singer, record producer	High school
Hank Williams	U.S. singer–songwriter	High school
Lucinda Williams	U.S. singer–songwriter	High school
Eric Wright	Rap artist	High school
Tammy Wynette	U.S. singer–songwriter	High school
Neil Young	Canadian singer–songwriter	High school
	Comedians	
Cliff Arquette	Created the character Charley Weaver	High school
Roseanne Barr	*Roseanne Bar Show*	High school
Jack Benny	Vaudeville, radio, early television	High school
Joey Bishop	Comedy writer, straight man	High SChool
Carol Burnett	*Carol Burnett Show*	College
George Burns	Vaudeville, radio, television	High school
Eddie Cantor	Vaudeville, television	Elementary school
George Carlin	Stand-up, television	High school
Billy Connolly	Scottish stand-up and sketch comic	High school
Bill Cosby	Stand-up; *I Spy, The Cosby Show*	High school
Ellen DeGeneres	Stand-up; *Ellen*	College
Redd Foxx	Stand-up; *Sanford and Son*	High school
Jackie Gleason	*The Honeymooners*	High school
Whoopi Goldberg	Stand-up, television, film	High school
Benny Hill	*Benny Hill Show*	High school
D.L. Hughley	Stand-up, television	High school
Kevin James	*The King of Queens*	College
Alan King	Stand-up, television, film	High school
George Kirby	*The George Kirby Show*	High school
Jerry Lewis	Slapstick stand-up, film, television	High school
Groucho Marx	Marx Brothers	Elementary school
Rosie O'Donnell	Stand-up, television, film	College
Paula Poundstone	Comedy writer, stand-up, television	High school
Richard Pryor	Stand-up, television, film	High school
Gilda Radner	*Saturday Night Live*	College
Chris Rock	Stand-up, film	High school
Red Skelton	Vaudeville, stage, radio, television, film	Elementary school
Tracey Ullman	*The Tracey Ullman Show*	High school

Name	Reminder	Dropped Out
	The Performing Arts (*continued*)	
	Comedians (*continued*)	
Damon Wayans	Wayans Brothers Productions	High school
Keenan Ivory Wayans	Wayans Brothers Productions	College
Marlon Wayans	Wayans Brothers Productions	College
Flip Wilson	*The Flip Wilson Show*	High school
Ernie Wise	U.K. television comic, *Morecambe and Wise*	High school
	Illusionists	
David Copperfield	Made the Statue of Liberty disappear	College
Harry Houdini	Escape artist	High school
James Randi	Escape artist	High school
Howard Thurston	Entertained over 60 million people before 1932	Elementary school
	Actors	
Don Adams	*Get Smart*	High school
Danny Aiello	*Moonstruck*	High school
Jack Albertson	*Days of Wine and Roses*	High school
Anthony Andrews	*Haunted*	High school
Dan Aykroyd	*Ghostbusters*	College
Lew Ayres	*Of Mice and Men*	College
Kevin Bacon	*Mystic River, Footloose*	High school
Sean Bean	*National Treasure*	High school
Warren Beatty	*Bonnie and Clyde, Dick Tracy*	College
Jean-Paul Belmondo	*Hold-Up, Les Misérables*	High school
Orlando Bloom	*The Lord of the Rings*	High school
Humphrey Bogart	*Casablanca*	High school
Marlon Brando	*A Streetcar Named Desire, The Godfather*	High school
Charles Bronson	*Death Wish*	High school
Pierce Brosnan	*The Thomas Crown Affair*	High school
Raymond Burr	*Perry Mason*	High school
James Caan	*The Godfather*	High school
Sebastian Cabot	*Family Affair*	High school
Nicolas Cage	*Leaving Las Vegas, Gone in Sixty Seconds*	High school
James Cagney	*Yankee Doodle Dandy, Mr. Roberts, Ragtime*	College
Michael Caine	*Alfie, The Man Who Would Be King*	High school
Keith Carradine	*Nashville, Will Rogers Follies, Deadwood*	College
Jim Carrey	*Ace Ventura Pet Detective, Liar Liar*	High school
Charlie Chaplin	*Modern Times*	Elementary school
Maurice Chevalier	*Gigi*	High school
Sean Connery	*Goldfinger, The Rock, The Avengers*	High school
Noel Coward	*Around the World in 80 Days, The Italian Job*	Elementary school
Michael Crawford	*Phantom of the Opera*	High school
Russell Crowe	*Gladiator*	High school
Tom Cruise	*Mission Impossible*	High school
Matt Damon	*Good Will Hunting*	College
Jeff Daniels	*Dumb and Dumber*	College
Robert De Niro	*Taxi Driver, Raging Bull, Analyze This*	High school
James Dean	*Rebel without a Cause*	College
Reginald Denny	*Batman*	High school

Millionaire Dropouts

The Performing Arts (*continued*)

Actors (*continued*)

Name	Reminder	Dropped Out
Gerard Depardieu	*Green Card, The Man in the Iron Mask*	Elementary school
Johnny Depp	*Edward Scissorhands, Pirates of the Caribbean*	High school
Leonardo Di Caprio	*Titanic*	High school
Vin Diesel	*Saving Private Ryan, XXX*	College
Matt Dillon	*The Flamingo Kid, There's Something about Mary*	High school
Brad Dourif	*The Lord of The Rings*	College
Robert Downey Jr.	*Chaplin; Good Night, and Good Luck.*	High school
Charles Durning	*O Brother, Where Art Thou*	High school
Rupert Everett	*My Best Friend's Wedding*	High school
Peter Facinelli	*The Scorpion King*	College
Colin Farrell	*Daredevil*	High school
Errol Flynn	*Captain Blood, The Adventures of Robin Hood*	High school
Ben Foster	*The Laramie Project, Hostage*	High school
Michael J. Fox	*Back to the Future*	High school
Jamie Foxx	*Ray*	College
Clark Gable	*Gone with the Wind*	High school
James Garner	*Maverick, The Rockford Files, The Great Escape*	High school
Richard Gere	*Pretty Woman*	College
Topher Grace	*That 70's Show*	College
Cary Grant	*She Done Him Wrong, To Catch a Thief, Charade*	High school
Gene Hackman	*Bonnie and Clyde, The Birdcage, Heist*	High school
Tom Hanks	*Forrest Gump*	College
Ethan Hawke	*Training Day*	College
Sterling Hayden	*Dr. Strangelove*	High school
Dustin Hoffman	*The Graduate, Tootsie, Rain Man*	College
Paul Hogan	*Crocodile Dundee*	High school
Bob Hope	*Road to Rio, The Seven Little Foys, Spies Like U.S.*	High school
Bob Hoskins	*Enemy of the State*	High school
Djimon Hounsou	*Gladiator*	College
Joshua Jackson	*Dawson Creek*	High school
Michael Keaton	*Beetlejuice, Batman*	College
Harvey Keitel	*Thelma and Louise, Pulp Fiction*	High school
Chris Klein	*American Pie*	College
Yaphet Kotto	*Homicide*	High school
Ashton Kutcher	*That 70's Show*	College
Jude Law	*The Talented Mr. Ripley, The Aviator*	High school
Heath Ledger	*Brokeback Mountain*	High school
Jason Lee	*Chasing Amy, Mallrats*	High school
Jarod Leto	*Panic Room*	High school
Tobey Maguire	*Spider-Man*	High school
Evan Marriot	*Joe Millionaire*	High school
Steve Martin	*The Jerk, Roxanne, Shopgirl*	College
Lee Marvin	*Cat Ballou, The Dirty Dozen, M Squad*	High school
Ewan McGregor	*Star Wars*	High school
Steve McQueen	*The Great Escape*	High school
Robert Mitchum	*Cape Fear*	High school
Yves Montand	*Z; On a Clear Day, You Can See Forever*	Elementary school

APPENDIX

Name	Reminder	Dropped Out
	The Performing Arts *(continued)*	
	Actors (continued)	
Roger Moore	*Live and Let Die, For Your Eyes Only*	High school
Donny Most	*Happy Days*	College
Bill Murray	*Groundhog Day, Ed Wood, Lost in Translation*	College
Dustin Nguyen	*21 Jump Street*	College
Peter O'Toole	*Lawrence of Arabia*	High school
Al Pacino	*The Godfather*	High school
Joe Pesci	*Goodfellas*	High school
Joaquin Phoenix	*Gladiator*	High school
Brad Pitt	*A River Runs Through It, Mr. and Mrs. Smith*	College
Donald Pleasance	*Halloween*	High school
Sidney Poitier	*A Raisin in the Sun, In the Heat of the Night, Jackal*	Elementary school
Dennis Quaid	*Any Given Sunday*	College
Anthony Quinn	*Zorba the Greek, The Guns of Navarone*	High school
Anthony Rapp	*Rent*	College
Keanu Reeves	*Matrix*	High school
Burt Reynolds	*Smokey and the Bandit*	College
Roy Rogers	*The Roy Rogers Show*	High school
Charlie Sheen	*Platoon, Hot Shots, Two and a Half Men*	High school
Christian Slater	*Broken Arrow, The Contender, Alone in the Dark*	High school
Kevin Sorbo	*Hercules*	College
Kevin Spacey	*L.A. Confidential, American Beauty, K-PAX*	High school
Sylvester Stallone	*Rocky*	College
Rod Steiger	*The Pawnbroker, Doctor Zhivago*	High school
Patrick Stewart	*Dune, Lady Jane, L.A. Story*	High school
Eric Stoltz	*Fast Times at Ridgemont High*	High school
Danny Thomas	*The Danny Thomas Show*	High school
John Travolta	*Saturday Night Fever, Grease, Pulp Fiction*	High school
Peter Ustinov	*Spartacus, Topkapi, Alice in Wonderland*	High school
Jean-Claude Van Damme	*Time Cop*	High school
Ken Wahl	*Wise Guy*	High school
Mark Wahlberg	*Boogie Nights, Four Brothers*	High school
Clint Walker	*Dirty Dozen*	High school
Bruce Willis	*Die Hard*	College
Anson Wilson	*Happy Days*	College
Owen Wilson	*Meet the Parents, Wedding Crashers*	High school
Paul Winfield	*Terminator*	College
Elijah Wood	*Lord of the Rings*	High school
James Woods	*Casino*	College
	Actresses	
Julie Andrews	*My Fair Lady, Mary Poppins, The Sound of Music*	High school
Christina Applegate	*Married…with Children*	High school
Courtney Cox Arquette	*Friends*	College
Lucille Ball	*I Love Lucy*	High school
Brigitte Bardot	*And God Created Woman, Helen of Troy*	High school
Drew Barrymore	*E.T., Scream, Riding in Cars with Boys*	High school
Kate Beckinsale	*Pearl Harbor*	College

Name	Reminder	Dropped Out
	The Performing Arts (*continued*)	
	Actresses (*continued*)	
Karen Black	*Five Easy Pieces*	High school
Clara Bow	*Wings*	High school
Louise Brooks	*The Canary Murder Case*	High school
Ellen Burstyn	*The Last Picture Show; Same Time, Next Year*	High school
Neve Campbell	*Scream*	High school
Jill Clayburgh	*An Unmarried Woman*	College
Toni Collette	*The Sixth Sense*	High school
Joan Crawford	*What Ever Happened to Baby Jane?*	High school
Beverly D'Angelo	*Vegas Vacation*	High school
Majandra Delfino	*Traffic*	High school
Bo Derek	*10, Bolero*	High school
Cameron Diaz	*There's Something About Mary, Charlie's Angels*	High school
Patty Duke	*The Miracle Worker*	High school
Jeanne Eagels	*Jealousy*	High school
Carrie Fisher	*Star Wars, The Blues Brothers, When Harry Met Sally*	High school
Tara Fitzgerald	*Like Father Like Son*	College
Eva Gabor	*Gigi*	High school
Greta Garbo	*Grand Hotel, Anna Karenina, Ninotchka*	High school
Jennie Garth	*Beverly Hills 90210*	High school
Lillian Gish	*Miss Susie Slagle's, The Unforgiven*	College
Susan Hampshire	*The Forsyte Saga, The Grand*	High school
Margaux Hemingway	*Lipstick, Dangerous Cargo*	High school
Helen Hunt	*As Good As It Gets*	College
Iman	*L.A.Story*	High school
Angelina Jolie	*Girl, Interrupted; Gone in Sixty Seconds*	High school
Nicole Kidman	*Eyes Wide Shut, Moulin Rouge!, Cold Mountain*	High school
Eartha Kitt	*St. Louis Blues, Batman, Fatal Instinct*	High school
Jennifer Jason Leigh	*Fast Times at Ridgemont High*	High school
Juliette Lewis	*Natural Born Killers*	High school
Heather Locklear	*Spin City*	College
Traci Lords	*Growing Pains*	High school
Sophia Loren	*Desire Under the Elms, Two Women*	Elementary school
Andie MacDowell	*Groundhog Day, Multiplicity*	College
Jena Malone	*Cold Mountain*	High school
Sophie Marceau	*The World Is Not Enough*	High school
Vanessa Marcil	*Las Vegas*	High school
Kelly McGillis	*Top Gun*	High school
Eva Mendes	*Hitch*	College
Alyssa Milano	*Charmed*	High school
Tina Modotti	*The Tiger's Coat*	Elementary school
Marilyn Monroe	*The Seven Year Itch, The Misfits*	High school
Demi Moore	*Ghost, Disclosure*	High school
Meg Mullally	*Will and Grace*	College
Julie Newmar	*Seven Brides For Seven Brothers*	College
Cathy Podewell	*Dallas*	College
Sarah Polley	*Dawn Of The Dead*	High school
Teri Polo	*Meet the Fockers*	High school

APPENDIX

Name	Reminder	Dropped Out
	The Performing Arts *(continued)*	
	Actresses (continued)	
Leah Remini	*The King of Queens*	High school
Michelle Rodriguez	*S.W.A.T.*	High school
Theresa Russell	*Black Widow*	High school
Rene Russo	*Tin Cup, The Thomas Crown Affair*	High school
Roselyn Sanchez	*Rush Hour 2*	College
Catya Sassoon	*Inside Out*	High school
Alicia Silverstone	*Clueless*	High school
Sharon Stone	*Basic Instinct, Casino*	College
Hilary Swank	*Million Dollar Baby*	High school
Uma Thurman	*Kill Bill*	High school
Marisa Tomei	*My Cousin Vinny*	College
Twiggy	*The Blues Brothers*	High school
Susan Ward	*Shallow Hal*	High school
Estella Warren	*Driven*	High school
Naomi Watts	*Mulholland Drive, The Ring*	High school
Mae West	*She Done Him Wrong, My Little Chickadee*	High school
Kate Winslet	*Titanic*	High school
Catherine Zeta-Jones	*Chicago*	High school
	Sports	
	Team Sports	
Willy Aybar	Los Angels Dodgers	High school
Yogi Berra	Yankees	High school
Roberto Clemente	Pittsburgh Pirates	High school
Joe DiMaggio	New York Yankees	High school
Miura Kazuyoshi	Soccer player, Japanese National Team	High school
Tommy Lasorda	Baseball team manager	High school
Tommy Nunez	Basketball referee	High school
Bobby Orr	Boston Bruins	High school
William Owens	NLBPA–Memphis	Elementary school
Pelé	Brazilian soccer player	Elementary school
Joe Pepitone	New York Yankees	High school
Manny Ramirez	Boston Red Sox	High school
Derek Sanderson	New York Rangers	High school
Sammy Sosa	Baltimore Orioles	High school
Casey Stengel	New York Mets	High school
Miguel Tejada	Oakland Athletics	High school
Fernando Valenzuela	St. Louis Cardinals	High school
	Individual Sports	
Mario Andretti	Race car driver	Elementary school
Boris Becker	Tennis player	High school
Bjorn Borg	Tennis player	High school
Jennifer Capriati	Tennis player	High school
Dale Earnhardt	Stock car driver	High school
Nick Faldo	Golfer	High school

MILLIONAIRE DROPOUTS

Name	Reminder	Dropped Out

Sports (continued)

Individual Sports (continued)

Name	Reminder	Dropped Out
Gigi Fernández	Tennis player	College
Scott Fischer	Climber	High school
George Foreman	Boxer	High school
A.J. Foyt	Race car driver	High school
Joe Frazier	Boxer	High school
Laird Hamilton	Surfer	High school
Thomas Hearns	Boxer	High school
Larry Holmes	Boxer	Elementary school
David L. Jackson	Boxer	High school
Tony Jacklin	Golfer	High school
Jean-Claude Killy	Skier	High school
Rod Laver	Tennis player	High school
Joe Louis	Boxer	High school
Brian Orser	Ice skater	High school
Floyd Patterson	Boxer,	High school
Mary Lou Retton	Gymnast	High school
Chi Chi Rodriguez	Golfer	High school
Paul P-Rod Rodriguez	Skateboarder	High school
Gene Sarazen	Golfer	Elementary school
Willie Shoemaker	Jockey	High school
Jackie Stewart	Race car driver	High school
Alberto Tomba	Skier	High school
Lee Trevino	Golfer	High school
Ron Turcotte	Jockey	High school
Ian Woosnam	Golfer	High school
Mildred "Babe" Zaharias	Olympic gold medalist, star of multiple sports	High school

Give the gift of Millionaire Dropouts™ to your friends, family and business associates

Order here and we will ship for free

☐ YES, I want _____ copies of *Millionaire Dropouts: Inspiring Stories of the World's Most Successful Failures* at $16.95 each.

☐ YES, I want _____ copies of *Millionaire Dropouts High School Edition: Never Let Your Schooling Interfere with Your Education* at $12.95 each.

☐ YES, I want _____ copies of *Millionaire Dropouts College Edition: Why Dropping Out Might Be the Best Decision You Ever Made* at $14.95 each.

☐ YES, I want _____ copies of *Millionaire Dropouts Parents Edition: Why You Should Support Your Child Who Wants to Drop Out* at $16.95 each.

☐ YES, I want _____ copies of *Millionaire Dropouts Biography Edition: Biographies of the World's Most Successful Failures* at $16.95 each.

☐ YES, I want _____ copies of *Millionaire Dropouts Mini-Book: Words of Wisdom* at $6.95 each.

☐ YES, I want _____ copies of *Millionaire Dropouts Mini-Book: Innovators* at $6.95 each.

☐ YES, I want to receive my FREE subscription to Millionaire Dropouts electronic monthly newsletter. My email address is listed below.

☐ YES, I am interested in having Woody Woodward speak to my organization. Please contact me with details.

Please charge my:
☐ Visa ☐ Master Card ☐ American Express ☐ Discover

Credit card number _____

Expiration date (month/year) _____/_____

Name _____

Organization _____

Title _____

Address _____

_____

City _____ State _____Zip _____

Phone _____ Fax _____

Email (please print clearly) _____

Signature _____

Privacy Policy: We hate junk mail as much as you therefore we don't send any.

Three ways to order

1. Return completed form to:

        D.U. Publishing
        39252 Winchester Road #107-430
        Murrieta CA 92563

2. Order online at www.MillionaireDropouts.com

3. Fax orders to 951-346-3280